COOKBOOK FOR TEENS

This Book Includes:

Baking and Dessert Cookbook.

190 Easy-to-Follow Sweet and

Savory Recipes for Young Cooks

Vicky Cooper

Legal & Disclaimer

The information contained in this book and its contents is not designed to replace or take the place of any form of medical or professional advice; and is not meant to replace the need for independent medical, financial, legal or other professional advice or services, as may be required. The content and information in this book has been provided for educational and entertainment purposes only.

The content and information contained in this book has been compiled from sources deemed reliable, and it is accurate to the best of the Author's knowledge, information and belief. However, the Author cannot guarantee its accuracy and validity and cannot be held liable for any errors and/or omissions. Further, changes are periodically made to this book as and when needed. Where appropriate and/or necessary, you must consult a professional (including but not limited to your doctor, attorney, financial advisor or such other professional advisor) before using any of the suggested remedies, techniques, or information in this book.

Upon using the contents and information contained in this book, you agree to hold harmless the Author from and against any damages, costs, and expenses, including any legal fees potentially resulting from the application of any of the information provided by this book. This disclaimer applies to any loss, damages or injury caused by the use and application, whether directly or indirectly, of any advice or information presented, whether for breach of contract, tort, negligence, personal injury, criminal intent, or under any other cause of action.

You agree to accept all risks of using the information presented inside this book.

You agree that by continuing to read this book, where appropriate and/or necessary, you shall consult a professional (including but not limited to your doctor, attorney, or financial advisor or such needed) before using any of the suggested remedies, techniques, or information in this book.

Table of Contents: Baking Cookbook for Teens

Table of Contents: Dessert Cookbook for Teens

BAKING COOKBOOK FOR TEENAGERS

Recipe Book for Easy, Quick and Tasty Dishes for Beginners Kids 9-12 and Teenagers to Enjoy with the Whole Family

Vicky Cooper

Introduction

The Basics Of Baking

Baking is all about precise measurements, cooking times and temperatures, and doneness cues (signs that your baked goods are done) can spell the difference between success and failure in baking.

Baking recipes, in general, rely heavily on five categories of ingredients:

- **Fat:** Butter, vegetable shortening, oil, cream, cheese

- **Flavoring ingredients:** Chocolate, fruit, vanilla (and other flavored) extract, spices like cinnamon, ginger, and nutmeg

- **Flours:** Wheat flours (all-purpose flour, bread flour, pastry flour, cake flour) as well as wheat-free flours like rice flour or almond flour

- **Leaveners (things that make baked goods rise):** Baking powder, baking soda, eggs, yeast

- **Sweeteners:** Granulated sugar, brown sugar, confectioners' (or powdered) sugar, molasses, honey, maple syrup

Of these ingredients, flour is the one most commonly associated with all sorts of baking—sweet or not.

Baking Skills

Self-drive

First things first, whether you bake to feed yourself or want to share the baking skills, you must want to do it.

Organization

The most prominent and successful chefs know that baking is a juggling act. It requires you to have your bakery prepared with everything including premeasured ingredients and baking appliances close at hand.

Attention to detail

As I have mentioned earlier, baking is an act of science that highly relies on temperature and precise measurements.

Communication

Assuming that you are in a commercial bakery, having clear communication with fellow bakers is extremely important.

Composure under pressure

Sometimes things can really heat up especially in a busy bakery which may not necessarily be as a result of a fast cooking oven but sometimes the workload.

Curiosity and creativity

For you to be a successful baker you need to combine science and art. You need to consistently come up with new crowd-pleasing pastries.

Patience and dedication

Baking is a well-calculated process where every step count. Some steps in pastry may seem of less significance or time consuming but they are the most vital.

Baking Techniques

Preheating oven

ovens need to be hot before you start baking.

Preparing baking pan or tin

There is nothing intimidating like a falling off cake when trying to get it out of the baking dish. To avoid disappointments from your precious treat, line the pan with parchment paper or generously grease the base and sides of the pan with butter.

Measuring ingredients

Baking is more scientific than the general cooking and that is why the ratio of ingredients should be strictly measured as stated on the recipe.

Rubbing in

The secret behind a light, crisp pastry to make short crust pastry, scones or scrambles is to get the butter coat as much flour as possible.

Creaming method

Just like whisking eggs, creaming is a way of incorporating air in the baking goods making the mixture fluffier and lighter.

Whisking eggs

Just like the creaming method, this is a way of getting air into your creation making it fluffier and lighter.

Equipments

Take this list into the kitchen and do a quick inventory of what you already have.

Baking dish

Baking sheet (aka cookie sheet)

Cake pan

Colander

Cookie cutter

Cookie scoop

Cutting board

Double boiler

Offset spatula

Parchment paper

Pastry brush

Pastry cutter (or pastry blender)

Pie plate or pie dish

Pie weights

Piping (or pastry) bag

Piping tips

Ramekin

Rubber spatula

Rolling pin

Saucepan

Sieve

Silicone mat

Skillet (frying pan)

Springform pan

Tart pan

Tube pan (or angel food cake pan)

Whisk:

Wire rack:

Electric mixer

Food processor

Loaf pan

Measuring cups and spoons

Terminology

Baking, like any other specialty, has a language of its own. Here is a list of the baking terms you'll see in this book, along with their definitions. See the pages referenced for more details where appropriate.

- **Beat** - Stir two or more ingredients together using a handheld electric mixer, a stand mixer, or a spoon

- **Blind bake** - Prebake or partially bake a pie crust before adding a filling

- **Cream together -** Beat air into butter or another fat. Butter and sugar are often creamed together.

- **Cut in** - Use a pastry cutter, knife, or food processor to cut butter or shortening into a bowl of flour until distributed in the flour

- **Divided -** Used in the ingredient list to indicate that the ingredient is added to the recipe at two or more different times, thus the quantity is "divided." For example, if a recipe calls for "1 cup of oil, divided" in the ingredient list, the instructions might tell you to use ½ cup in step 1 and the remaining ½ cup later in the recipe.

- **Dollop -** Drop by heaping spoonful.

- **Fold in -** Mix gently with a rubber spatula to combine one ingredient into another without deflating or releasing any air.

- **Grease** - Coat a baking pan with butter, shortening, cooking spray, or oil.

- **Knead** - Work dough, with either your hands or an electric mixer, to develop the gluten in the flour.

- **Let rise** - Give yeasted bread dough time for the yeast to consume the sugar, ferment it, and release the gas that will make the bread become airy.

- **Mix** - Combine two or more ingredients by stirring, whisking, or beating.

- **Sift** - Shake flour or other powdered ingredients through a sieve to remove lumps.

- **Stir** - Use a spoon or rubber spatula to mix two or more ingredients.

- **Whip** - Whisk a liquid (such as cream or egg whites) rapidly in order to fill it with air (see here).

- **Whisk** - Beat air into liquid or dry ingredients like eggs or flour.

Measuring

By now you know that in cooking, you can often wing it with ingredients, throwing in a splash of this or a pinch of that as the urge strikes, but baking is an exact science. If you don't have the right combinations and proportions of ingredients, your cake or cookies could end up being a total flop. It is essential to use proper measuring techniques in baking.

Measuring Dry Ingredients

- Measuring by weight (ounces and pounds) is the most precise way to measure dry ingredients, but since most recipes (in the United States) use volume measurements (cups, teaspoons, and tablespoons), follow these tips for the most accuracy:

- Measure larger quantities of dry ingredients in scoop-shaped measuring cups (usually made of plastic or metal). Fill the cup so that the ingredient is mounded over the top edge, and then level off the top with the flat side of a knife.

- When measuring very light ingredients like flour or cornstarch, use the "spoon-and-level" method to avoid packing the ingredient too tightly into the measuring cup (giving you more of the ingredient than required): Spoon the ingredient from the container into the measuring cup until it is mounded up over the brim, and then level it off with the flat side of a knife.

- Scoop up larger grainy ingredients like sugar using the measuring cup and then level off the top using the flat edge of a knife or just by shaking the excess off. Brown sugar is always (unless otherwise noted) measured "packed," which means it is pressed into the measuring cup so that it is firm and there is little space between the grains.

- Use measuring spoons to measure dry ingredients in quantities smaller than ¼ cup.

Measuring Wet/Liquid Ingredients

- When measuring liquid in ¼-cup or larger quantities, use transparent measuring cups (usually made of glass) placed flat on the counter. Pour the liquid into the measuring cup slowly. Get down to eye level with the cup and stop pouring when the level of liquid is at the desired measurement line.

- Use measuring spoons to measure liquids in teaspoon or tablespoon quantities. Fill the spoon so that the liquid comes up to the top edge and is flat across the top.

Mixing

You might not think that the act of mixing would require its own section, but there are actually a surprising number of ways to combine ingredients together, and sometimes your results are largely dependent on choosing the right one. Here are the most common mixing terms you'll see:

Beating

Stirring ingredients together using a handheld electric mixer, a stand mixer, or a spoon.

Creaming

You'll notice that many baking recipes begin with "cream together the butter and sugar" or a similar instruction. This is a way of mixing the butter and sugar together to create a light, fluffy structure for cakes and other baked goods. The process of creaming is used to combine fat (like butter or shortening) with sugar by beating them together. But creaming isn't as much about mixing the two ingredients together as it is about aerating the fat, or filling it with air. By folding the butter (or fat) over and over in the beating process, you create tiny air bubbles in it. Grains of sugar cut into the fat and magnify this effect.

Cutting in

Cutting in means combining fat (such as butter or shortening) with flour. The purpose of cutting in is to distribute pea-size bits of fat throughout the dough. This technique is used in making pastries like pie crusts, scones, and biscuits. In the high heat of the oven, the fat melts, creating steam, which makes air pockets in the dough. It's the secret to flaky pastry crust!

You can cut in using a food processor, pastry cutter, the back of a fork, or two knives. Whichever method you choose, always start with fat that is very cold and cut into small pieces.

To use a food processor: Fit the processor with the steel S blade. Put the flour in the bowl of the processor, and add the butter or other fat. Pulse the processor repeatedly until the mixture is in pea-size crumbs or a coarse meal.

To do it by hand: Place the flour in a mixing bowl, and toss the cold butter pieces on top. Use a pastry cutter, fork, or two knives to smash and/or slice the butter into smaller and smaller bits until you have a mixture of flour and butter in pea-size clumps.

Conversion Table

Volume Equivalents (Liquid)

STANDARD	US STANDARD (OUNCES)	METRIC (APPROXIMATE)
2 TABLESPOONS	1 FL. OZ.	30 ML
¼ CUP	2 FL. OZ.	60 ML
½ CUP	4 FL. OZ.	120 ML
1 CUP	8 FL. OZ.	240 ML
1½ CUPS	12 FL. OZ.	355 ML
2 CUPS OR 1 PINT	16 FL. OZ.	475 ML
4 CUPS OR 1 QUART	32 FL. OZ.	1 L
1 GALLON	128 FL. OZ.	4 L

Volume Equivalents (Dry)

STANDARD	METRIC (APPROXIMATE)
⅛ TSP	0.5 ML
¼ TSP	1 ML
½ TSP	2 ML
¾ TSP	4 ML
1 TSP	5 ML

1 TBSP	15 ML
¼ CUP	59 ML
⅓ CUP	79 ML
½ CUP	118 ML
⅔ CUP	156 ML
¾ CUP	177 ML
1 CUP	235 ML
2 CUPS OR 1 PINT	475 ML
3 CUPS	700 ML
4 CUPS OR 1 QUART	1 L

Oven Temperatures

FAHRENHEIT (F)	CELSIUS (C) (APPROXIMATE)
250°	120°
300°	150°
325°	165°
350°	180°

Table of Contents

Weight Equivalents

STANDARD	METRIC (APPROXIMATE)
½ OUNCE	15 G
1 OUNCE	30 G
2 OUNCES	60 G
4 OUNCES	115 G
8 OUNCES	225 G
12 OUNCES	340 G
16 OUNCES OR 1 POUND	455 G

Chapter 1: Easy Breakfast Recipes

1. Breakfast Toast Cups

Preparation Time: 20 Minutes

Cooking Time: 15 Minutes

Servings: 6

Ingredients

- 6 bread slices
- 2 tbsp butter
- Spinach, large handful
- 1/4 cup cheese
- 6 eggs
- 6 cooked bacon slices
- Pepper and salt to taste

Directions:

1. Preheat an oven to 375°F. In the meantime, lightly spray 6 muffin tin cups with butter. Roll out bread slices using a rolling pin making them rather thin. Cut out circles, 4-5inch, from each bread slice corner. Preserve the bread scraps. Half the circles and spray each with butter. Place a small bread scrap into the bottom of each muffin tin. Make sure it covers ⅔ of the tin bottom. Place 2 bread circles halves into each cup. Position them leaving minimal holes. Divide and load the remaining ingredients among the 6 muffin tins with egg going last. Bake in your oven for about 15 minutes until egg whites are set and thoroughly white. Remove from the oven and splash with pepper and salt. Immediately serve and enjoy.

Nutrition

Calories 290 kcal; Fat 20 g; Carbs 14 g; Sodium 630 mg; Protein 13 g

2. Breakfast Baked Potatoes

Preparation Time: 15 Minutes

Cooking Time: 1 Hour

Servings: 4

Ingredients

- 4 cleaned russet potatoes, large
- 1 tbsp black pepper
- 1 tbsp salt
- 1 cup cheddar cheese, shredded
- 4 large eggs
- 6 chopped crispy bacon strips
- 2 tbsp chives, chopped

Directions:

1. Preheat your oven to 425°F. Bake your potatoes for about 45-50 minutes until fork tender. Remove and let cool slightly. (Alternatively, microwave the potatoes for about 15-20 minutes until fork tender.) Cut a round opening on each potato top and remove it. Scoop most of the center out using a spoon. Place the boats on a baking sheet

then splash each with pepper and salt. Splash each with little cheese and crack an egg to each potato boat. Top with bacon then more cheese over the eggs. Bake for about 10-15 minutes until egg whites are set but still runny yolks.

2. Remove and splash with chives. Serve warm.

Nutritional Information

Calories 360 kcal; Fat 14 g; Carbs 39 g; Sodium 850 mg; Protein 18 g

3. Super Easy Banana Muffins

Preparation Time: 15

Cooking Time: 25

Servings: 10

Ingredients

- 2 large bananas
- 1/2 cup sugar, granulated
- 1/3 cup canola oil
- 1/2 tbsp vanilla extract
- 1/4 cup sugar, light brown
- 1 egg, large
- 1 tbsp cinnamon
- 1-1/ 2cups all-purpose flour
- 1/2 tbsp baking soda
- 1/2 tbsp salt
- 1 tbsp baking powder

Directions:

1. Preheat your oven to 425°F. In a 12-cavity muffin pan, line 10 cavities with cupcake liners. Place mashed bananas, granulated sugar, canola oil, vanilla, brown sugar, and egg in a mixing bowl, large, then

vigorously whisk until combined and smooth. Add cinnamon, flour, baking soda, salt, and baking powder to the mixing bowl and continue whisking until combined. Be careful to over-mix. Divide equally the mixture among the cupcake liners then place the muffin pan to your oven. Bake for about 5 minutes at 425°F. Now reduce temperature to 350°F and continue to bake for about 14-16 minutes until a toothpick comes out clean when inserted. Remove the muffin pan and let cool for about 5 minutes. Serve and enjoy!

Nutrition

Calories 210 kcal; Fat 8 g; Carbs 30 g; Sodium 250mg; Protein 3 g

4. Cheesy Baked Eggs

Preparation Time: 5 Minutes

Cooking Time: 15 Minutes

Servings: 1

Ingredients:

- 1 tbsp softened butter
- 2 tbsp milk, half and half or cream
- 2 large eggs
- Pinch of black pepper
- Pinch of salt
- 2 tbsp cheddar cheese, shredded

- 1 tbsp parmesan cheese, grated

Directions:

1. Preheat your oven to 400°F. In the meantime, coat inside of an oven ramekin, 8-ounces, with butter. Whisk milk and eggs in a bowl, small. Stir in pepper, salt, and cheeses. Pour the batter into the ramekin. Bake for about 15-18 minutes until eggs are cooked through. Let cool for about 5 minutes and serve. Enjoy!

Nutritional Information

Calories 358 kcal; Fat 28 g; Carbs 2 g; Protein 22 g; Sodium 450 mg

5. Eggs Baked in Avocado

Preparation Time: 5 Minutes

Cooking Time: 20 Minutes

Servings: 4

Ingredients

- 2 extra-large avocados
- Black pepper
- Salt
- 4 eggs

Directions:

1. Preheat your oven to 400°F.

2. Half the avocados and discard the pits. Now scoop out avocado flesh from each half. Leave 1/2 -inch flesh border in the skin then reserve scooped out flesh.

3. Arrange the halves in a baking dish, square, with cut side up.

4. Splash cavities with pepper and salt then crack an egg carefully into each half.

5. Season with pepper and salt to taste.

6. Bake for about 15-20 minutes on the oven middle rack until egg whites are set.

7. Make sure eggs are done then remove from the oven.

8. Serve immediately.

Nutritional Information

Calories 240 kcal; Fat 20 g; Carbs 11 g; Protein 9 g; Sodium 270 mg

6. Lemon Poppy Seed Baked Oatmeal

Preparation Time: 10 Minutes

Cooking Time: 25 Minutes

Servings: 8 Minutes

Ingredients

- 3 cups rolled oats, old-fashioned
- 3 eggs, large
- 2 cups vanilla almond milk, unsweetened
- 1/4 cup honey
- 1/4 tbsp Meyer lemon juice, fresh
- 1 tbsp Meyer lemon zest
- 1 tbsp vanilla extract, pure
- 1/4 tbsp salt
- 1 tbsp baking powder
- 1 tbsp poppy seeds

Directions:

1. Preheat your oven to350°F then lightly grease a baking, medium. Set aside. Mix all the ingredients together in a bowl, medium, until well combined. Transfer into the baking dish. Bake for 20-25 minutes in the oven while uncovered. Enjoy!

Nutritional Information

Calories 204 kcal; Fat 2.9 g; Carbs 34 g; Protein 3.5 g; Sodium 240 mg

7. Mixed Berry Vanilla Baked Oatmeal

Preparation Time: 15 Minutes

Cooking Time: 35 Minutes

Servings: 6-8

Ingredients

- 3 cups rolled oats, old-fashioned
- 1 tbsp salt
- 1-1/2 tbsp baking powder
- 3 cups fresh berries
- 2 lightly beaten eggs
- 2 tbsp pure vanilla extract
- 1/2 cup pure maple syrup
- 2-1/2 cups vanilla almond milk, unsweetened
- 3 tbsp butter, unsalted

Directions

1. Preheat your oven to 350°F.

2. Grease a 3-quart baking dish and set aside.

3. Combine oats, salt, and baking powder in a bowl then place half of the mixture into the baking dish.

4. Top with half of the berries then add the remaining mixture.

5. Whisk eggs, vanilla, maple syrup, almond milk, and butter in a mixing bowl then pour over oats.

6. Top with remaining berries then shake your baking dish forth and back, from side to side. This is to allow wet mixture to move down to the oats.

7. Bake for about 25-40 minutes uncovered until mixture is set and oats are tender.

8. Serve immediately with a milk splash. (alternatively, cool, cover and then refrigerate to reheat later)

Nutritional Information

Calories 267 kcal; Fat 8 g; Carbs 42 g; Protein 6 g; Sodium 304 mg

8. Baked Frittata

Preparation Time:15 Minutes

Cooking Time: 35 Minutes

Servings: 12

Ingredients:

- 1 cup deli ham, chopped
- 1-1/2 cups asparagus, chopped
- 1 chopped orange bell pepper
- 1 small chopped onion
- 2-1/2 mushrooms, chopped
- 1 cup cheddar cheese, shredded
- 12 eggs
- Dash of pepper, freshly-ground
- 1 tbsp garlic powder
- Dash of salt

Direction

1. Preheat your oven to 375°F. Meanwhile, grease a 9x13 pan with butter, coconut oil or oil. Add ham, asparagus, bell pepper, onion, mushrooms, and cheese to the pan. Quickly whisk eggs, pepper, garlic powder, and salt until combined well. Pour the mixture over vegetables in the pan and stir everything together until eggs fill crevices around meat and vegetables. Bake for about 25-35 minutes until frittata center is cooked through. Make sure a toothpick gets out clean when inserted in the center.
2. Serve and enjoy.

Nutritional Information

Calories 151 kcal; Fat 9 g; Carbs 5 g; Protein 11 g; Sodium 264 mg

9. French Toast Bake

Preparation Time: 15 Minutes

Cooking Time: 45 Minutes

Servings: 8

Ingredients

- 1 loaf sourdough bread, cubed
- 8 eggs
- 1/2 cup heavy cream
- 2 cups milk
- 2 tbsp vanilla
- 3/4 cup sugar

Toppings

- 1/2 cup flour
- 1 tbsp cinnamon
- 1/2 cup brown sugar
- 1/4 tbsp salt
- 1/2 cup butter cold pieces

Directions:

1. Evenly place sourdough bread cubes in a 9x13 pan, greased. Mix eggs, heavy cream, milk, vanilla, and sugar in a medium bowl then evenly

pour over bread cubes. Cover with saran wrap and place it in a fridge overnight. Mix flour, cinnamon, brown sugar, and salt in a bowl, medium, then place in butter pieces until crumbly. Place the mixture in a bag, Ziploc, and place in the fridge overnight. Now splash crumbly mixture over the bread evenly. Bake for about 45-60 minutes at 350°F until done.

2. Serve and enjoy.

Nutrition

Calories 580 kcal; Fat 24 g; Carbs 74 g; Protein 15 g; Sodium 563 mg

10. Baked Eggs and Spinach in Sweet Potato Boats

Preparation Time: 5

Cooking Time: 1 Hour & 15 Minutes

Servings: 4

Ingredients

- 2 sweet potatoes, large
- Pepper and salt
- 1 tbsp butter
- 1 cup finely chopped baby spinach, packed
- 4 eggs

Directions:

1. Preheat an oven to 400ºF. Bake sweet potatoes for about 45-60 minutes in the oven. Halve each sweet potato and scoop most of its flesh out leaving a small flesh rim round the potato skin. Season each half with pepper and salt. Add butter cubes to each potato half then top with spinach. Season again with pepper and salt. Break an egg carefully into each half. Bake the potato halves in your preheated oven for about 15 minutes until the eggs cook to your liking. Lastly, season once more with pepper and salt.
2. Serve and enjoy.

Nutritional Information

Calories 159 kcal; Fat 7 g; Carbs 17 g; Protein 7 g; Sodium 216 mg

11.Ham Hash Brown Casserole

Preparation Time: 30 Minutes

Cooking Time: 1 Hour

Servings: 16

Ingredients:

- Cooking spray
- ¼ cup all-purpose flour
- 4 cups milk, divided
- 1 cup mozzarella cheese, shredded
- 1 cup cheddar cheese, shredded
- Pepper to taste
- 2 cups deli ham, sliced into cubes
- 3 cups peas
- 10 cups hash browns, shredded

Directions:

1. Preheat your oven to 375 degrees F. Coat your baking pan with oil. Combine the flour and ½ cup milk in a bowl. Pour the remaining milk into a pan over medium heat and simmer for 2 minutes while stirring. Stir in the flour mixture. Simmer for 5 minutes. Turn off the heat. Stir in the mozzarella and cheddar. Season with the pepper. Mix the ham, peas and hash browns in a bowl. Pour the mixture into a baking pan. Cover with the foil and bake for 50 minutes. Remove the foil and bake for 3 to 5 minutes or until the surface has turned golden.

Nutrition

Calories 192 kcal; Fat 7g; Carbohydrates 21g; Protein 11g; Sodium 372mg

12. Breakfast Casserole

Preparation Time: 30 Minutes

Cooking Time: 1 Hour

Servings: 6

Ingredients:

- 2 teaspoons olive oil
- 1 cup button mushrooms, sliced
- 1 red sweet pepper, chopped
- 1 onion, chopped
- 8 oz. baguette bread, sliced into cubes
- 6 oz. smoked turkey sausage, sliced thinly
- ½ cup Swiss cheese, shredded
- 4 eggs
- 3 egg whites
- 1 teaspoon dried oregano, crushed
- 2 cups nonfat milk

Directions

1. In pan over medium heat, add the oil and cook the onion, mushrooms and sweet pepper for 5 minutes.

2. Spray your baking pan with oil. Then arrange half of the bread slices in the pan. Top with half of the mushrooms, half of the sausage and half of the cheese.

3. Repeat the layers. In a bowl, beat eggs and egg whites. Stir in the oregano and milk. Pour this mixture on top of the casserole.

4. Preheat your oven to 350 degrees F. Bake in the oven for 50 minutes.

5. Let it cool around 10 minutes before slicing and serving.

Nutrition

Calories 285 kcal

Fat 11.5 g

Carbohydrates 25 g

Protein 21.8 g

Sodium 533 mg

Table of Contents

Chapter 2: Easy Lunch Recipes

13. Bang Bang Shrimp

Preparation time: 10 Minutes

Cook time: 10 Minutes

Servings: 4

Ingredients:

Fixings

- 1 cup Almond flour
- ½ cup Parmesan
- ½ teaspoon Kosher Salt
- ¼ teaspoon Pepper
- 1-pound Jumbo Shrimp, stripped and deveined
- 1 Egg, beaten

Sauce

- ½ cup Mayo
- 1 tablespoon Sriracha Juice or 1 Lime

- 2 tablespoons Rice vinegar
- 1 teaspoon Garlic powder
- 2 tablespoons Soy sauce
- 2 tablespoons Swerve

Directions:

1. Include almond flour, Parmesan, salt, and pepper to a nourishment processor and heartbeat until it takes after coarse pieces. Dump into a shallow bowl. Plunge each shrimp in the beaten egg and afterward coat in the morsels, Place in a solitary layer noticeable all-around a fryer. You may need to cook in 2 clumps. Cook noticeable all-around fryer at 360F for 4 minutes, at that point, turn up the temperature to 400F and cook for 4 additional minutes. In the event that your shrimp are little, you should diminish the cooking time. To make the sauce, place all fixings in a medium bowl and race to join. Coat each shrimp with the sauce and serve.

Nutrition:

Calorie: 840 kcal

Fat: 65 g

Carbs: 38 g

Sodium: 2,190 mg

Protein: 26 g

14.Bacon Wrapped Stuffed Mushrooms

Preparation Time: 10 Minutes

Cooking Time: 15 Minutes

Servings: 10

Ingredients

- 4 oz. Cream cheese
- 10 Strips of bacon
- 6 Chives
- 1/4 tsp Garlic powder
- 10 Medium sized portobello mushrooms

Directions:

2. Set your stove on medium heat and placed pan on stove and keep cream cheese at cooking area for slightly melted. Clean mushrooms from stems by pulling out through hand and wash with water so that look like bowls. Keep mushrooms and bacon in the pan. Cook mushrooms in bacon grease for more extra flavor as this is my secret. You may cook them separately with little olive oil or butter on mushrooms. It takes 10-15 minutes on stovetop. Whenever it goes ready, prepare your stuffing with washing and chopping your chives then mix it with cream cheese in bowl and sprinkle in garlic powder and start stirring. If cooked then keep mushrooms on a plate and stuff cream cheese mixture into underside of mushrooms with the help of spoon, right into same bowl. If stuffing complete, wrap a single slice of bacon around each mushroom. Use toothpick to keep everything together if needed as it is depending upon size of mushrooms.

Nutrition:

Calorie: 14. Kcal; Fat: 0.5 g; Carbs: 0.6 g; Sodium: 78.2 mg; Protein: 1.7 g

15.Delicious Oven Fried Cod

Preparation Time: 10 Minutes; Cooking Time: 30 Minutes

Servings: 4

Ingredients:

- COD fillets, (or whatever fish you want to use - for thicker fish, increase baking time)
- 1/2 c shredded parmesan (not the powdered kind)
- 1 Tbsp dried, minced onions
- 1/2 c corn meal
- 1/2 tsp pepper
- 1/2 tsp garlic salt
- 1 tsp ground, paprika
- 1/2 tsp salt

Directions:

1. Preheat oven to 400-degree F. Line a shallow baking pan with foil. Spray with non- stick cooking spray or wipe with oil, as so fish won't stick. In a shallow dish, add seasonings, corn meal, and cheese and stir to combine. Dip each piece of fish into the milk, let excess drip off. Press each side into the crumbs (making sure well coated.) Place on sheet pan. Bake for 25 - 30 minutes or until nice and golden and fish is flaky. If using bigger pieces of fish, you may need to increase breading ingredients and baking time. Serve with lemon and tartar sauce. Enjoy!

Nutrition:

Calorie: 184 kcal; Fat: 1.7 g; Carbs: 11 g; Sodium: 170 mg; Protein: 28.4 g

16.Baked Pineapple Salmon

Preparation Time: 10 Minutes; Cooking Time: 30 Minutes

Servings: 4

Ingredients:

- Kosher salt
- 3 tbsp. melted butter
- 3 tbsp. sweet chili sauce
- 3 cloves garlic, minced
- 1 large salmon fillet (about 3 lbs)
- 2 tsp. freshly ground black pepper
- 17 pineapple rings, fresh or canned
- 2 tbsp. freshly chopped cilantro

Directions:

1. Preheat oven to 350°. Line a large rimmed baking sheet with foil and grease with cooking spray. In the center of the foil, lay pineapple slices in an even layer. Season both sides of the salmon with salt and pepper and place on top of pineapple slices. In a small bowl, whisk together butter, chili sauce, cilantro, garlic, ginger, sesame oil, and red pepper flakes. Brush all over salmon fillet. Bake until the salmon is cooked through, about 25 minutes. Switch the oven to broil, and broil for 2 minutes, or until fish is slightly golden.

2. Garnish with sesame seeds and green onions and serve with lime wedges.

Nutrition:

Calorie: 313.7 kcal; Fat: 6.4 g; Carbs: 23.7 g; Sodium: 199.1 mg; Protein: 36.6

17. Baked Shrimp Scampi

Preparation Time: 5 Minutes

Cooking Time: 15 Minutes

Servings: 4

- **Ingredients**
  1 cup butter
- 2 tablespoons Dijon mustard
- 1 tablespoon fresh lemon juice
- 1 tablespoon chopped garlic
- 1 tablespoon chopped fresh parsley
- 2 pounds medium raw shrimp, shelled, deveined, and thawed if frozen

Directions

1. Preheat oven to 450 degrees F. Combine the butter, mustard, lemon juice, garlic, and parsley in a small saucepan and stir over low heat until melted and blended. Remove from heat.
2. Arrange shrimp in a single layer in a large shallow baking dish. Pour the butter mixture over the shrimp and gently stir the shrimp to make sure all are coated. Bake in a 450 degrees F oven for 12 to 15 minutes or until the shrimp are pink, curled, and opaque.
3. Serve immediately.

Nutrition:

Calorie: 135 kcal; Fat: 8.6 g; Carbs: 11 g; Sodium: 109 mg; Protein: 3.5 g

18. Baked Chicken Spaghetti Squash

Preparation Time: 1 Hour

Cooking Time: 40 Minutes

Servings: 8

Ingredients:

- 3 lb. spaghetti squash
- 4 cups broccoli florets, steamed
- 1 tablespoon vegetable oil
- 1 onion, chopped
- ½ teaspoon dried thyme
- Pepper to taste
- 2 cloves garlic, crushed and minced
- 10 oz. mushrooms, sliced
- 20 oz. low sodium cream of mushroom soup
- 1 ½ lb. chicken breast fillet, chopped
- ½ cup cheddar cheese, shredded

Directions

1. Preheat your oven to 375 degrees F. Spray your baking pan with oil. Slice the squash lengthwise, then remove the seeds.
2. Microwave on high for 12 minutes. Scrape the flesh and transfer to a plate. Set aside. Pour the oil in a pan over medium heat. Cook the mushrooms for 8 minutes.
3. Add the onion and cook for another 8 minutes. Add the thyme, pepper and garlic. Cook for 30 seconds, stirring. Stir in the squash, broccoli, and chicken. Pour the mixture into the baking pan.
4. Top with the cheddar. Cover with foil. Bake in the oven for 25 minutes. Remove the foil. Bake for another 10 minutes.

5. Let cool before serving.

Nutrition

Calories: 273kcal; Fat: 11g; Carbohydrates: 18g; Protein: 25g; Sodium: 493mg

19. Shrimp Casserole

Preparation Time: 30 Minutes

Cooking Time: 1 Hour

Servings: 6

Ingredients:

- 6 corn tortillas, sliced into strips
- ½ cup light sour cream
- 1 cup green salsa
- 3 tablespoons all-purpose flour
- 4 oz. grated Monterey Jack cheese
- 4 tablespoons fresh cilantro, chopped and divided
- 12 oz. shrimp, cooked, peeled and deveined
- 1 tomato, chopped
- 1 cup corn kernels

Directions

1. Preheat your oven to 350 degrees F. Arrange half of the tortilla strips in a baking dish. In a bowl, mix the sour cream, salsa, flour, cheese and cilantro.
2. In another bowl, mix the shrimp, tomatoes and corn kernels. Top the tortillas with the sour cream mixture, and then with the shrimp mixture. Repeat layers.
3. Bake in the oven for 40 minutes.

Nutrients per Serving:

Calories 242 kcal; Fat 8g; Carbohydrates 25g; Protein 20g; Sodium 564mg

20. Turkey Broccoli Casserole

Preparation Time: 30 Minutes

Cooking Time: 10 Minutes

Servings: 8

Ingredients:

- 1 tablespoon vegetable oil
- 1 lb. chicken breast fillet, trimmed
- 4 cups low-fat milk, divided
- ¼ cup all-purpose flour
- 3 cups broccoli florets
- 4 cups cooked brown rice
- 2 cups low-fat cheddar cheese, shredded
- Salt and pepper to taste
- Crispy fried onions

Directions

1. Preheat your oven to 400 degrees F. Pour the oil in a pan over medium high heat.

2. Cook the chicken for 5 minutes per side. Transfer to a cutting board. Slice into cubes. In a bowl, combine half of the milk and flour. Add the remaining milk to the pan. Bring to a boil. Slowly add the flour and milk mixture. Keep boiling while stirring for 2 minutes.

3. Add the broccoli and rice. Cook for 2 minutes. Stir in the cheese and chicken. Season with the salt and pepper. Add the onions on top. Transfer the skillet to the oven. Bake for 10 minutes.

4. Let cool before serving.

Nutrition

Calories 353; Fat 13.1 g; Carbohydrates 30.8 g; Protein 24.6 g; Sodium 413 mg

21.Chicken Cashew Casserole

Preparation Time: 40 Minutes

Cooking Time: 20 Minutes

Servings: 6

Ingredients:

- Cooking spray
- ¼ cup hoisin sauce
- 1 cup low-sodium chicken broth
- 4 teaspoons cornstarch
- 2 tablespoons freshly grated ginger
- Pepper to taste
- ½ teaspoon red pepper flakes
- 1 lb. chicken breast fillet, sliced into strips
- 2 onions, sliced into wedges
- 6 cloves garlic, crushed and minced
- ½ cup cashews
- 2 stalks celery, sliced
- 1 green sweet pepper, chopped
- 1 cup chow-mein noodles, coarsely broken
- 2 cups bok choy, sliced
- 2 carrots, sliced
- 2 cups brown rice, cooked
- ¼ cup green onions, chopped

Directions

1. Preheat your oven to 400 degrees F. Spray your baking pan with oil. In a bowl, mix the hoisin sauce, chicken broth, cornstarch, ginger, pepper and red pepper flakes. Set aside. Spray your pan with oil. Put it over medium heat. Cook the chicken until brown on both sides. Transfer to a plate.

2. Add the onions, garlic, celery, sweet pepper, bok choy and carrots in the pan. Cook for 4 minutes. Pour in the sauce. Cook for 3 minutes. Put your chicken back to the pan along with the cooked rice. Transfer the mixture to the baking pan.

3. Cover with foil. Bake for 20 minutes. Remove the foil. Sprinkle the cashews and noodles on top. Bake for another 5 minutes.

4. Garnish with the green onions and serve.

Nutrition

Calories 340 kcal

Fat 10.1 g

Carbohydrates 40.4 g

Protein 22.9 g

Sodium 480 mg

22. Pork Chops with Fresh Pumpkin, Apple, and Cinnamon

Preparation Time: 15 Minutes; Cooking Time: 19 Minutes

Servings:4

Ingredients:

- 2 tablespoons olive oil
- 1 tablespoon fresh thyme leaves
- 2 teaspoons ground cinnamon
- 2 pounds bone-in pork chops (about 2 inches thick)
- 1-pound fresh pumpkin, peeled, seeded, and large diced (see substitution tip)
- 2 apples (I like Fuji for this), peeled, cored and roughly chopped

Directions:

1. Preheat the oven to 450°F. Line a sheet pan with aluminum foil. Place the pan into the oven to preheat. In a small bowl, stir together the olive oil, thyme, and cinnamon. Rub half the oil mixture onto the pork chops. Remove the pan from the oven and place the pork chops on it. Return the pan to the oven for 5 minutes. While the pork chops cook, in a large bowl, toss the pumpkin and apples with the remaining oil mixture until coated. Remove the pan from the oven. Flip the pork chops (they should have started to brown). Add the pumpkin and apples to the pan in an even layer. Bake for 12 to 14 minutes more, or until the pork chops register an internal temperature of 145°F on a meat thermometer.

Nutrition:

Calorie: 471 kcal; Fat: 23 g; Carbs: 26 g; Sodium: 943 mg; Protein: 40 g

Table of Contents

Chapter 3: Snack Recipe

23.Yogurt Banana Bread

Preparation Time: 20 Minutes

Cooking Time: 60 Minutes

Servings: 12

Ingredients

- Butter, for greasing the pan
- Flour, for dusting the pan
- 1⅔ cups all-purpose flour
- 1 teaspoon baking soda
- ½ teaspoon cinnamon
- ½ teaspoon table salt
- 2 large eggs, at room temperature
- ¾ cup granulated sugar
- 1½ cups mashed, very ripe bananas (3 to 5 bananas)
- ½ cup vegetable or canola oil
- 2 tablespoons plain Greek yogurt

- 1 teaspoon vanilla extract

Directions:

1. Preheat the oven to 350°F. Lightly grease and flour a loaf pan. Mix the dry ingredients. In a medium bowl, mix together the flour, baking soda, cinnamon, and salt until well combined. Mix remaining ingredients.

2. In another medium bowl, beat together the eggs and sugar for 3 to 5 minutes, or until light and fluffy.

3. Stir in the banana, oil, yogurt, and vanilla until just combined. Combine the ingredients. Make a well in the center of the dry ingredients. Pour the wet ingredients into the well.

4. Stir until just combined. Bake the bread. Pour the batter into the prepared loaf pan.

5. Bake at 350°F for 45 to 60 minutes, or until a toothpick inserted in the center comes out clean.

Nutrition:

Calorie: 72.9 kcal

Fat: 1.9 g

Carbs: 12.9 g

Sodium: 144.9 mg

Protein: 1.2 g

24.Coconut Macaroons

Preparation time: 10 minutes

Cooking time: 40 minutes

Servings: 4

Ingredients:

- 1 egg white
- 3 cups coconut flakes
- 2/3 cup almond milk
- ½ teaspoon vanilla extract
- 1 teaspoon lemon juice
- 1 teaspoon lemon zest
- For the lemon curd:
- 5 tablespoons ghee, softened
- ½ cup raw honey
- 2 egg yolks
- 2 eggs
- 1 teaspoon lemon zest, grated
- 2/3 cup lemon juice

Directions:

1. In a bowl, mix honey with ghee and stir with a mixer for 3 minutes. Add 2 egg yolks and 2 eggs and mix again well. Add 2/3 cup lemon juice and mix 1 minute more.

2. Transfer this to a saucepan, heat up over medium-low heat and cook for 15 minutes stirring often. Add 1 teaspoon lemon zest, stir, take off heat, transfer to a bowl and keep in the fridge for now. In a bowl, mix coconut flakes with almond milk, 1 egg white, vanilla extract, 1 teaspoon lemon juice, 1 teaspoon lemon zest and stir well.

3. Shape small cookies, arrange them on a lined baking sheet, place in the oven at 325 degrees F and bake 20 minutes. Take cookies out of the oven, leave aside for 5 minutes and arrange them on a platter.

4. Fill each macaroon with the lemon curd you've made and serve. Enjoy!

Nutrition:

Calorie: 638 kcal

Fat: 50 g

Carbs: 47 g

Fiber: 6.4 g

Protein: 8.2 g

25.Zebra Marble Cake

Preparation Time: 30 Minutes

Cooking Time: 45 Minutes

Servings: 8

Ingredients

- Butter, for greasing the pan
- Flour, for dusting the pan
- 2 cups all-purpose flour
- 2 teaspoons baking powder
- ¼ teaspoon table salt
- 1 cup granulated sugar
- 4 large eggs, at room temperature
- 1 cup vegetable or canola oil
- 1 cup milk (2 percent or whole)
- 1 teaspoon vanilla extract
- 3 tablespoons sifted unsweetened cocoa powder

Directions

1. Preheat the oven to 350°F. Grease and flour a 9-inch round cake pan. Mix the dry ingredients. In a medium bowl, stir together the flour, baking powder, and ¼ teaspoon of salt. Blend the sugar and eggs. In

a large bowl, beat together the granulated sugar and eggs with an electric mixer on medium until well blended, about 2 minutes.

2. Add the oil, 1 cup of milk, and 1 teaspoon of vanilla, beating until well blended. Combine the ingredients. Add the flour mixture to the egg mixture, beating on medium until just blended. Make the chocolate batter.

3. Spoon half of the batter into a separate bowl. Whisk the cocoa powder into one of the bowls, stirring to blend. Assemble the cake. To make stripes, alternate adding the two batters to the pan. Spoon about 3 tablespoons of vanilla batter into the center of the pan. Then spoon about 3 tablespoons of chocolate batter in the middle of the pan on top of the vanilla batter.

4. Repeat until all the batter is in the pan. The cake batter will spread to the edge of the pan as you add more. Bake the cake. Bake for 30 to 45 minutes, or until a toothpick inserted into the middle comes out clean.

5. Let the cake cool slightly in the pan, then remove from the pan and place on a wire rack to finish cooling.

Nutrition:

Calorie: 22.5 kcal

Fat: 8.4 g

Carbs: 34.5 g

Sodium: 135.5 mg

Protein: 3.5 g

26. Upside-Down Apple Cupcakes

Preparation Time: 30 Minutes; Cooking Time: 20 Minutes

Servings: 18

Ingredients

- Butter, for greasing the pans

For the Apples

- 4 tablespoons unsalted butter
- ⅔ cup brown sugar
- 2 large apples, cored, peeled, and very thinly sliced

For the Cakes

- 1 cup all-purpose flour
- 1¼ teaspoons baking powder
- ½ teaspoon cinnamon
- ¼ teaspoon table salt
- ½ cup (1 stick) unsalted butter, at room temperature
- 1 cup granulated sugar
- 1 large egg
- 1 teaspoon vanilla extract
- ¼ cup buttermilk

Directions:

Table of Contents

1. Preheat the oven to 350°F. Generously grease 18 cups of 2 (12-cup) muffin pans. Cook the apples. In a medium skillet over medium heat, heat 4 tablespoons of butter and the brown sugar, stirring until combined and melted.

2. Add the apples, stirring to combine, and cook for 4 to 5 minutes or until the apples are soft, stirring occasionally. Spoon 2 or 3 apple slices and a little sauce into the bottom of each muffin cup. Mix the dry ingredients. In a medium bowl, stir together the flour, baking powder, cinnamon, and salt.

3. Cream the butter and sugar. In a large bowl, beat ½ cup of room-temperature butter with an electric mixer on medium speed for about 10 seconds, or until smooth. Beat in the granulated sugar until well blended and light and fluffy, about 2 minutes.

4. Add the eggs, one at a time, beating after each egg is added, then beat in the vanilla. Combine the ingredients. In batches, alternate adding the flour mixture and the buttermilk to the butter mixture, beating on low after each addition until the batter is just combined. Bake the cupcakes.

5. Spoon the batter over the apples in the muffin cups until half to ⅔ full. Bake for 18 to 20 minutes, or until a toothpick inserted into the center comes out clean.

6. Cool slightly, then gently flip the cakes over onto a platter or serving plate.

Nutrition:

Calorie: 118.45 kcal; Fat: 3.8 g; Carbs: 20.15 g; Sodium: 123 mg; Protein: 2.1 g

27.Zucchini Cupcakes

Preparation Time: 20 Minutes

Cooking Time: 40 Minutes

Servings: about 1-1/2 dozen.

Ingredients:

- 3 large eggs
- 1-1/3 cups sugar
- 1/2 cup canola oil
- 1/2 cup orange juice
- 1 tsp. almond extract
- 2-1/2 cups all-purpose flour
- 2 tsps. ground cinnamon
- 2 tsps. baking powder
- 1 tsp. baking soda
- 1 tsp. salt
- 1/2 tsp. ground cloves
- 1-1/2 cups shredded zucchini

Frosting:

1. 1 cup packed brown sugar

2. 1/2 cup butter, cubed
3. 1/4 cup 2% milk
4. 1 tsp. vanilla extract
5. 1-1/2 to 2 cups confectioners' sugar

Directions:

Set the oven at 350° and start preheating. Whisk together the first five ingredients. Mix dry ingredients together; slowly put into the egg mixture and blend properly. Mix in zucchini. Fill 2/3 of each of paper-line muffin cups with the batter. Bake for 20-25 minutes, or till a toothpick comes out clean when inserted into the center. Allow to cool for 10 minutes. Take away and place on a wire rack. Mix milk with butter and brown sugar in a large saucepan for frosting. Boil over medium heat; cook while stirring for 1-2 minutes, or till thickened. Take away from the heat; mix in vanilla. Allow to cool to lukewarm. Slowly whisk in confectioner' sugar till the frosting achieves spreading consistency. Frost the cupcakes.

Nutrition:

Calories: 327 kcal

Carbohydrate: 52 g

Fat: 12 g

Protein: 3 g

Sodium: 305 mg

28. Walnut Fudgy Brownies

Preparation Time: 10 Minutes

Cooking Time: 45 Minutes

Servings: 6 dozen.

Ingredients:

- 2 cups sugar
- 3/4 cup baking cocoa
- 1/2 tsp. baking soda
- 2/3 cup vegetable oil, divided
- 1/2 cup boiling water
- 1-1/3 cups all-purpose flour
- 1 tsp. vanilla extract
- 1/4 tsp. salt
- 2 eggs
- 1 cup chopped walnuts

Directions:

Mix baking soda, cocoa, and sugar in a bowl. Add water and 1/3 cup of oil, whisk until smooth. Whisk in the rest of the oil, eggs, salt, vanilla, and flour. Mix in walnuts. Spread the mixture into the greased 13x9-inch baking pan. Bake it at 350° until the toothpick will come out clean once you insert it into the center, about 35-40 minutes. Put on a wire rack to cool. Slice into bars.

Nutrition:

Calories: 63 kcal; Carbohydrate: 8 g; Fat: 3 g; Protein: 1 g; Sodium: 19 mg

29. Walnut-coconut Coffee Cake

Preparation Time: 10 Minutes

Cooking Time: 55 Minutes

Servings: 12-15

Ingredients:

- 1 cup vegetable oil
- 1 cup sugar
- 1 cup packed brown sugar
- 2 large eggs
- 1 tsp. vanilla extract
- 2-1/2 cups all-purpose flour
- 1 tsp. baking soda
- 1 tsp. salt
- 1 tsp. ground cinnamon
- 1 cup buttermilk
- 1 cup sweetened shredded coconut
- 1 cup chopped walnuts
- Confectioners' sugar, optional

Directions:

1. Mix together the vanilla, eggs, sugars and oil well in a big bowl. Mix cinnamon, salt, baking soda and flour together; put to egg mixture alternating with buttermilk. Mix till just moisten. Mix in walnuts and coconut till just combined. Put in a 13x9-inch greased baking pan; bake for 45-55 minutes at 350° till an inserted toothpick in middle exits clean; cool down on a wire rack.

2. If desired, dust using confectioners' sugar.

Nutrition:

Calories: 410 kcal; Carbohydrate: 48 g; Fat: 22 g; Protein: 6 g; Sodium: 289 mg

30.Chocolate Chip Cookies

Preparation Time: 5 Minutes

Cooking Time: 15 Minutes

Servings: 16

Ingredients:

- 2¼ cups flour
- 1 tablespoon cornstarch
- 1 teaspoon baking soda
- ¾ teaspoon salt
- 1 cup vegan margarine
- ¾ cup brown sugar
- ¾ cup sugar
- ¼ cup water
- 1 tablespoon pure vanilla extract
- 1½ cups vegan chocolate chips

Directions:

1. Preheat the oven to 350 degrees. Line 2 or 3 large baking sheets with parchment paper.
2. In a medium bowl, whisk together flour, cornstarch, baking soda, and salt. Set aside.
3. Using a stand or hand mixer, beat the margarine, brown sugar, sugar, water, and vanilla until fluffy. Slowly beat in the flour mixture. Once the flour mixture is incorporated, add chocolate chips and pecans. Scoop about 1 rounded tablespoon of dough at a time onto the prepared baking sheets, leaving about 2 inches between each scoop. Bake for 10 to 12 minutes, or until the edges are golden.
4. Let cool on the pan and serve.

Nutrition:

Calorie: 171 kcal: Fat: 8.8 g; Carbs: 22 g; Sodium: 153 g; Protein: 2.5 g

31. Banana Bread Cobbler

Preparation Time: 20 Minutes; Cooking Time: 40 Minutes

Servings: 6

Ingredients

- 1 cup rolled oats
- ¾ cup brown sugar
- ½ cup flour
- ½ cup vegan margarine, softened

Cobbler

- 1 cup flour
- ⅔ cup sugar
- 1½ teaspoons baking powder
- ½ teaspoon salt
- 1 cup non-dairy milk
- ½ cup vegan margarine, melted
- 3 ripe bananas, sliced

Directions:

1. Preheat the oven to 375 degrees. Lightly grease an 8-inch square pan. To make the streusel topping: In a medium bowl, mix oats, sugar, flour, and margarine until crumbly. To make the cobbler, in a large bowl, whisk flour, sugar, baking powder, and salt until combined.
2. Stir in nondairy milk and melted margarine until just combined. Pour the batter into the prepared pan and arrange banana slices on top. Cover the bananas with the streusel topping and bake until golden brown, about 40 minutes, or until a toothpick inserted in the center comes out clean with a few crumbs clinging to it.
3. Serve warm or at room temperature with a scoop of vanilla ice cream, I you would like.

Nutrition:

Calorie: 490 kcal; Fat: 24 g; Carbs: 68 g; Sodium: 420 mg; Protein: 5 g

Chapter 4: Savory Pies Recipes

32.Chicken Sausage and Tomato Pie

Preparation Time: 10 Minutes

Cooking Time: 50 Minutes

Servings: 8

Ingredients

- 1 (10-inch) baked pie shell
- 2 tablespoons (30 ml) olive oil
- 1/2 cup (80 g) onion, chopped
- 8 oz. (250 g) chicken sausage, chopped
- 1 ½ cup (225 g) cherry tomatoes, halved
- 1/2 cup (30 g) fresh basil, chopped
- 3 ounces (85 g) cheddar cheese, grated
- 3/4 cup (185 g) light mayonnaise
- 2 tablespoons (30 g) Dijon mustard
- 1 teaspoon (5 ml) hot sauce
- Salt and freshly ground black pepper

Directions

1. Preheat and set your oven to 375 F (190 C). Place pie crust in a pie pan or round baking dish. Sauté the onions in oil for 2-3 minutes over medium flame.

2. Add the sausage; cook, stirring for 3-5 minutes. Add the tomato halves and fresh basil; cook for 3 minutes. Transfer the sausage mixture into the prepared pie crust.

3. Combine the cheese, mayonnaise, mustard, and hot sauce in a medium bowl. Mix well and pour over the sausage mixture.

4. Bake the pie in the oven for 30-35 minutes. Cool slightly before cutting into portions.

5. Serve and enjoy.

Nutrition

Calories - 325 kcal

Fat - 24.4 g

Carbs - 18.6 g

Protein - 8.9 g

Sodium - 557 mg

33. Homemade Tuna Pot Pie

Preparation Time: 10 Minutes

Cooking Time: 1 Hour & 10 Minutes

Servings: 6

Ingredients

- 2 tablespoons (30 ml) olive oil
- 1/2 cup (80 g) shallots, chopped
- 6 ounces (185 g) canned tuna flakes, drained
- 1 cup (150 g) frozen mixed vegetables
- 1 celery stalk (about 60 g), chopped
- 1/2 teaspoon (1 g) dried thyme
- 1/2 teaspoon (1 g) dried oregano
- 1 (10 oz. or 300 g) can cream of mushroom soup
- 1/3 cup (85 ml) milk
- 2 sheets of pastry dough
- Salt and freshly ground black pepper

Directions

1. Preheat and set your oven to 350 F (175 C). Heat oil in a skillet or pan over medium flame. Stir-fry shallots for 2 minutes. Add the tuna, mixed vegetables, celery, thyme, and oregano. Cook, stirring for 5-7 minutes. Remove from the heat source.

2. Flatten 1 pastry dough using a rolling pin, then cover the bottom and sides of a large baking dish. Set aside. Mix together the cream of mushroom soup and milk in a jug or bowl. Season with salt and pepper.
3. Transfer the tuna-vegetable mixture into the pie crust. Then, add the soup mixture on top.
4. Roll the remaining dough to make a flat sheet then cover the filling; seal the edges by pressing with a fork.
5. Bake in the oven for about 40 minutes or until cooked through. Cool slightly before cutting into portions.
6.   Serve and enjoy.

Nutrition

Calories - 305 kcal

Fat - 18.4 g

Carbs - 17.6 g

Protein - 12.9 g

Sodium - 524 mg

34. Homemade Chicken Pot Pie

Preparation Time: 10 Minutes

Cooking Time: 1 Hour & 10 Minutes

Servings: 8

Ingredients

- 1-pound (450 g) chicken breast fillet, diced
- 2 medium (60 g) carrots, diced
- 1 cup (150 g) green peas
- 1 stalk celery (about 60 g), diced
- 1/4 cup (60 g) melted butter
- 1/2 cup (80 g) onion, chopped
- 1/3 cup (40 g) flour
- 1/2 teaspoon (2.5 g) salt
- 1/4 teaspoon (0.5 g) ground black pepper
- 1 ½ cups (375 ml) chicken broth
- 3/4 cup (185 ml) milk
- 2 sheets pastry dough

Directions

1. Preheat and set your oven to 375 F (190 C). Using a rolling pin flatten one sheet of pastry and press at the bottom and the sides of a pie

pan or round baking dish. Bake in the oven for 10-12 minutes. Set aside.

2. Combine the chicken with the carrots, peas, and celery in a medium saucepan. Fill half of the saucepan with water and boil for 15 minutes. Remove from the heat and drain.

3. Cook the onion in butter, then add in the flour, salt, and pepper.

4. Stir in chicken broth and milk. Simmer over medium-low heat, stirring often until mixture becomes thick. Place the chicken mixture into the pie crust. Then pour the white sauce on top of it.

5. Using a rolling pin flatten the remaining pastry and cover the filling. Seal the edges and make slits on top to allow airflow. Bake the pie for 35-40 minutes.

6. Cool slightly before serving. Enjoy.

Nutritional Information:

Calories - 382 kcal

Fat - 15.3 g

Carbs - 36.8 g

Protein - 23.7 g

Sodium - 735 mg

35. Homemade Spanakopita

Preparation Time: 15 Minutes

Cooking Time: 1 Hour & 15 Minutes

Servings: 12

Ingredients

- 2 tablespoons (30 ml) olive oil
- 1 medium (110 g) onion, chopped
- 1/2 cup (30 g) green onions, chopped
- 2 cloves of garlic, minced
- 1-pound (450 g) spinach, chopped
- 1/2 cup (30 g) parsley
- 2 large eggs (about 60 g each)
- 3/4 cup (185 g) ricotta cheese
- 3/4 cup (150 g) feta cheese
- 8 sheets of phyllo dough
- Cooking oil spray

Directions

1. Preheat and set your oven to 350 F (175 C). Grease your baking sheet with oil spray. Heat olive oil in a skillet or pan over medium flame. Sauté the onion, the green onions, and garlic for 3 minutes. Then add in the spinach and parsley.

2. Cook for 2 more minutes then remove from heat to cool. Mix together the eggs, cheese, and the spinach mixture in a bowl. Put 1 sheet of dough in the baking pan.

3. Brush with olive oil and put another sheet on top. Repeat this process until you've got a thick piece.

4. Spread the spinach and the cheese mixture into the dough and fold the overhang over. Brush with oil and then layer with 4 more sheets of dough.

5. Bake for about 30 minutes then cut the Spanakopita into small squares or triangle.

6. Serve and enjoy.

Nutrition:

Calories - 193 kcal

Fat - 7.6 g

Carbohydrates - 24.1 g

Protein - 8.8 g

Sodium - 351 mg

36.Savory Lamb Pie

Preparation Time: 20 Minutes

Cooking Time: 1 Hour 20 Minutes

Servings: 8

Ingredients

- 3/4 cup (95 g) flour
- 1 teaspoon (5 g) salt
- 1 teaspoon (2 g) ground black pepper
- 1 1/2 pounds (675 g) lamb meat, diced
- 2 tablespoons (30 g) butter
- 2 tablespoons (30 ml) olive oil
- 3 medium yellow onions (about 110 g each), divided
- 8 cloves of garlic, minced
- 1/3 cup (85 g) tomato paste
- 1 tablespoon (3.5 g) fresh rosemary, chopped
- 1 teaspoon (2 g) dried thyme
- 2 sheets of pastry dough

Directions

1. Combine the salt and pepper with the flour in a large bowl then add the lamb meat. Toss to coat well.

2. Heat the butter and 2 tablespoons of olive oil in a large skillet or pan over medium flame. Brown the lamb in it for 5 to 7 minutes. Transfer to a bowl. Using the same pan, cook the minced onion until they caramelize.

3. Return the lamb into the pan and then add the garlic, tomato paste, rosemary, and thyme. Cook over medium-low heat for 5 minutes. Then, transfer to a baking dish.

4. Preheat and set your oven to 375 F (190 C). Flatten the pastry dough using a rolling pin and cover the baking dish with it. Seal the sides and remove excess.

5. Make slits in the middle for allowing air flow. Bake the pie for about 25-30 minutes or until cooked through and golden brown.

6. Cool slightly before serving. Enjoy.

Nutrition

Calories - 337 kcal

Fat - 20.0 g

Carbohydrates - 17.1 g

Protein - 22.6 g

Sodium - 197 mg

37. Homemade Shepherd's Pie

Preparation Time: 15 Minutes

Cooking Time: 1 Hour 15 Minutes

Servings: 8

Ingredients

- 1 1/2 pounds (675 g) potatoes
- 3/4 cup half and half cream
- 1/4 cup (60 g) melted butter
- 2 tablespoons (30 ml) olive oil
- 1 medium (110 g) onion, chopped
- 2 cups (300 g) frozen mixed vegetables, thawed
- 1 1/2 pounds (675 g) ground beef
- 1/2 cup (125 ml) beef broth
- 2 teaspoons (10 ml) Worcestershire sauce
- Salt and freshly ground black pepper

Directions

1. Peel and quarter the potatoes and put them in a pot. Cover with enough cold water and add some salt. Boil then lower heat to a

simmer and cook until tender, about 25 minutes. Drain the potatoes and transfer to a large mixing bowl.

2. Mash using a potato masher and then add half and half cream and butter. Mix well and season to taste.

3. Preheat and set your oven to 400 F (200 C). Heat oil in a pan or skillet over medium flame. Stir-fry onion for about 3 minutes. Add the beef and cook, stirring for 5-7 minutes.

4. Add the thawed mixed vegetables and season with salt and pepper. Stir in Worcestershire sauce and beef broth; cook for 10 more minutes. Transfer beef mixture into a baking dish and top with mashed potatoes.

5. Bake for about 25-30 minutes.

6. Then cool slightly and serve. Enjoy.

Nutrition

Calories - 377 kcal

Fat - 20.8 g

Carbohydrates - 18.1 g

Protein - 26.5 g

Sodium - 280 mg

38.Mini Meat and Vegetable Pie

Preparation Time: 10 Minutes

Cooking Time: 55 Minutes

Servings: 8

Ingredients

- 2 sheets of pastry dough
- 2 tablespoons (30 ml) olive oil
- 1 medium (110 g) onion, chopped
- 1 teaspoon (3 g) garlic, minced
- 1-pound (450 g) ground beef
- 1 cup (130 g) broccoli, chopped
- 1 medium (60 g) carrot, grated
- 1 (10 oz. or 300 g) can cream of mushroom soup
- 1/2 cup (125 ml) skim milk
- Salt and freshly ground black pepper
- Cooking oil spray

Directions

1. Preheat and set your oven to 375 F (190 C). Lightly grease a muffin pan with oil spray. Using a rolling pin, flatten the dough and cut into small circles.

2. Put 1 round pastry into each of the muffin cups. Firmly press so that it lays flat at the bottom and up to the sides.

3. Set aside. Heat the olive oil in a non-stick pan or skillet over medium flame. Stir-fry onion and garlic until aromatic, about 3 minutes.

4. Add the ground beef and cook for 5 minutes. Add the broccoli, carrot, cream of mushroom soup, and skim milk. Cook for about 5 minutes and season to taste.

5. Spoon the filling onto each muffin cup. Cover each with remaining pastry and prick the center with a fork.

6. Bake the pies for 25 to 30 minutes.

7. Then cool slightly before serving. Enjoy.

Nutrition

Calories - 218 kcal

Fat - 11.0 g

Carbohydrates - 9.8 g

Protein - 19.2 g

Sodium - 253 mg

39. Chicken and Cheese Quiche

Preparation Time: 10 Minutes; Cooking Time: 1 Hour 10 Minutes

Servings: 8

Ingredients

- 1 (10-inch) baked pie crust
- 2/3 cup (165 ml) skim milk
- 1 package of onion soup mix
- 1/4 cup (60 g) Parmesan cheese, grated
- 1 teaspoon (2 g) paprika
- 1 cup (140 g) cooked chicken fillet, shredded
- 3 ounces (85 g) Gruyere cheese, shredded
- 5 large eggs (about 60 g each)

Directions

1. Preheat and set your oven to 425 F (210 C). Place the pie crust in a pie pan or dish. Spread the chicken evenly and then top with Gruyere cheese. In a medium bowl, beat the eggs using a fork, then stir in the milk, soup mix, and Parmesan cheese. Pour this mixture over the chicken and then sprinkle paprika on top.

2. Bake the quiche in the oven for about 15 minutes, then lower the heat to 350 F (175 C) and bake for 30 minutes more or until completely set. Let it cool, about 10 to 12 minutes before cutting into portions. Serve and enjoy.

Nutrition

Energy - 319 kcal; Fat - 18.6 g; Carbohydrates - 15.9 g; Protein - 21.3 g; Sodium - 480 mg

Chapter 5: Pizza Recipe

40.Cauliflower Pizza Crust

Preparation Time: 10 Minutes

Cooking Time: 30 Minutes

Servings: 4

Ingredients:

- 0.5 tsp. salt
- 16 oz. cauliflower florets
- 1 large egg
- tbsp. coconut flour
- 3 tsp. avocado oil
- 0.5 tsp. Italian seasoning
- 1 tsp. coconut oil
- food blender
- large skillet
- large flat sheet or pizza pan

Directions:

1. Set your oven to heat at the temperature of 405° Fahrenheit. Pulse the cauliflower in a food blender for approximately 60 seconds until it is a crumbly consistency. Heat the coconut oil and cauliflower in a frypan for approximately 5 minutes as it becomes tender. Transfer the cauliflower to a kitchen towel and twist to eliminate the extra water. Repeat this step as many times as necessary to make sure the moisture has been eliminated. Prepare your pizza pan or flat sheet with a section of baking lining and set to the side. In a glass dish, blend the riced cauliflower, salt, egg, coconut flour, avocado oil, and Italian seasoning and integrate until it thickens.

2. Flatten the dough onto the prepped pan to no less than a quarter inch.

3. Heat for 25 minutes if then and up to half an hour if thicker.

4. Complete with your favorite toppings and finish in the stove for another 5 minutes.

Nutrition:

Calorie: 142.6 kcal

Fat: 10.7 g

Carbs: 2.6 g

Sodium: 202.2 g

Protein: 9.5 g

41.Mozzarella Pizza Crust

Preparation Time: 5 Minutes

Cooking Time: 20 Minutes

Servings: 4

Ingredients:

- cups mozzarella cheese, shredded
- 0.75 cup almond flour
- 1 whole egg
- 2 tbsp. cream cheese, full-fat
- 0.25 tsp. salt
- Pizza pan or large flat sheet

Directions:

1. Set your stove to heat at the temperature of 350° Fahrenheit. Use a microwave-safe dish to nuke the almond flour, mozzarella, and cream cheese for approximately 60 seconds until liquefied.
2. Toss the cheese and heat for an additional half minute.
3. Blend the salt and egg into the cheese for about half a minute. Place a section of baking lining on the counter and transfer the dough to the middle. Use another section of baking lining to place on top. Flatten to no less than a quarter of an inch.
4. Separate the top baking lining and transfer to the pan of choice. Heat for approximately 13 minutes until turning golden.

5. Layer with your toppings of choice and heat for about 5 minutes. Serve.

Nutrition:

Calorie: 290 kcal; Fat: 13 g; Carbs: 26 g; Sodium: 580 mg; Protein: 12 g

42. Pizza with Tomato and Mozzarella

Preparation Time: 15 minutes

Cooking Time: 9 to 18 minutes

Servings: 2

Ingredients:

For the Dough

- 8 g instant yeast
- 375 ml water
- 500 g all-purpose flour
- 10 g salt

For the Pizza Topping

- ¼ cup olive oil
- 1 (16 oz.) can crushed tomatoes
- 16 oz. fresh mozzarella
- Fresh basil
- Red pepper flakes

Directions:

1. Drizzle the olive oil around the crust of the pizza. Spread a light layer of crushed tomatoes over the dough, leaving the crust area bare.

2. Tear pieces of fresh mozzarella and arrange them around the dough. Scatter a handful of fresh basil leaves over the cheese and finish with

a sprinkling of red pepper flakes. Give your peel a little shake to make sure that your pizza is not sticking to the peel and will slide.

3. If the dough seems sticky, use a dough scraper to pull up the dough and scatter more flour under the pizza to help it along. Put your peel into the oven, aligning the far edge of the pizza with the far side of the pizza stone.

4. Give the peel a gentle nudge to help the far edge of the pizza start to slide onto the stone. Once it's in position, give your peel a brisk pull, and your pizza will slide fully onto the pizza stone.

5. Bake for anywhere from 9 to 18 minutes. Serve hot and enjoy!

Nutrition:

Calories: 1,523.50 kcal

Protein: 101 g

Fat: 30.19 g

Carbohydrates: 209.84 g

43. Four Cheese Margherita Pizza

Preparation Time: 20 Minutes

Cooking Time: 20 Minutes

Servings: 8

Ingredients:

• ¼ cup of extra virgin olive oil

• 1 Tbsp. of garlic, minced

• ½ tsp. of sea salt

• 8 Roma tomatoes, thinly sliced

• 12-inch pizza crusts, pre-baked

• 8 oz. of mozzarella cheese, shredded

• 4 oz of Fontina cheese, shredded

• 10 basil leaves

• ½ cup of Parmesan cheese, grated

• ½ cup of feta cheese, crumbled

Directions:

1. In a bowl, add in the extra virgin olive oil, minced garlic and dash of sea salt. Add in the tomatoes and toss well to mix. Cover and set aside to rest for 15 minutes. Heat up the oven to 400 degrees.
2. Brush the pizza crusts with the tomato mix. Sprinkle the shredded mozzarella and fontina cheese over the top.
3. Add a topping of the basil leaves, grated Parmesan cheese and crumbled feta cheese.
4. Place into the oven to bake for 10 minutes or until golden. Remove and serve immediately.

Nutrition:

Calorie: 551 kcal; Fat: 25.6 g; Carbs: 54.4 g; Sodium: 1183 mg; Protein: 28.9 g

44. Mexican Pizza

Preparation Time: 15 Minutes

Cooking Time: 30 Minutes

Servings: 8

Ingredients:

- ½ pound of ground beef
- 1 onion, chopped
- 1 clove of garlic, minced
- 1 Tbsp. of powdered chili
- 1 tsp. of ground chili
- ½ tsp. of smoked paprika
- Dash of black pepper
- 1, 16 ounce can have refried beans
- 4, 10-inch flour tortillas
- ½ cup of mild salsa
- 1 cup of cheddar cheese
- 1 cup of Monterey jack cheese
- 2 green onions, chopped
- 2 Roma tomatoes, chopped
- ¼ cup of jalapeno pepper, sliced thinly
- ¼ cup of sour cream, optional

Directions:

1. Heat up the oven to 350 degrees. Grease 2 pie plates with cooking spray. In a skillet set over medium to high heat, add in the ground beef, chopped onion and minced garlic. Stir well to mix.

2. Cook for 8 to 10 minutes or until browned. Drain the excess grease. Season with the powdered chili, ground cumin, smoked paprika, dash of salt and dash of black pepper.

3. Place a tortilla into the pie plates. Cover with a layer of beans. Spread half of the beef over the beans. Cover with a tortilla. Place into the oven to bake for 10 minutes.

4. Remove and set aside to cool. Spread half of the mild salsa over the tortillas. Sprinkle the shredded cheddar and Monterey jack cheese over the top.

5. Add half of the tomatoes, half of the chopped green onions and half of the jalapenos over the top.

6. Place into the oven to bake for 5 to 10 minutes.

7. Remove and cool for 5 minutes before serving.

Nutrition:

Calorie: 550 kcal

Fat: 30 g

Carbs: 49 g

Sodium: 980 mg

Protein: 21 g

45. Pickle Pizza

Preparation Time: 10 Minutes

Cooking Time: 20 Minutes

Servings: 4 – 6

Ingredients:

- 1 pizza crust
- 2 Tbsp. of extra virgin olive oil
- 1 tsp. of powdered garlic
- 1 tsp. of Italian seasoning
- 1 ½ cup of mozzarella cheese, shredded
- ¼ cup of Parmesan cheese, grated
- ½ cup of pickles, thinly sliced
- 1 Tbsp. of dill, chopped
- ½ tsp. of crushed red pepper flakes
- Ranch dressing, for serving

Directions:

1. Heat the oven to 375 degrees. Place a sheet of parchment paper onto a large baking sheet.
2. In a bowl, add in the olive oil, powdered garlic and Italian seasoning. Stir well to mix. Transfer the pizza crust onto a baking sheet. Brush the surface with the oil mix.
3. Top off with the shredded mozzarella cheese and grated Parmesan cheese. Place into the oven to bake for 15 minutes or until melted. Remove and top off with the pickle slices. Place back into the oven to bake for an additional 5 minutes.

4. Remove and serve with a garnish of chopped dill, crushed red pepper flakes and a drizzling of the Ranch dressing.

Nutrition:

Calorie: 284 kcal; Fat: 17 g; Carbs: 24.6 g; Sodium: 780 mg; Protein: 8,5 g

46. Pizza Nachos

Preparation Time: 10 Minutes

Cooking Time: 15 Minutes

Servings: 6 – 8

Ingredients:

- 1 bag of tortilla chips
- 2 cups of pizza sauce
- 3 cups of mozzarella cheese, shredded
- 1 green bell pepper, chopped
- 1 cup of miniature pepperoni
- ½ cup of black olives, thinly sliced
- ½ cup of grated Parmesan cheese
- Parsley, chopped and for garnish

Directions:

1. Heat up the oven to 375 degrees. Line a baking sheet with a sheet of aluminum foil. On the baking sheet, add half of the tortilla chips. Drizzle half of the pizza sauce over the tortilla chips.
2. Top off with half of the shredded mozzarella cheese, half of the miniature pepperoni, chopped green bell pepper, sliced black olives and grated Parmesan cheese.
3. Repeat this layer one more time. Place into the oven to bake for 15 minutes or until the cheese is fully melted. Remove.
4. Garnish the top with the parsley. Serve.

Nutrition:

Calorie: 489 kcal; Fat: 37 g; Carbs: 26.3 g; Sodium: 379 mg; Protein: 13.4 g

47. Classic New York Pizza

Preparation Time: 1 Hour

Cooking Time: 25 Minutes

Servings: 4

Ingredients:

- 1 tsp. of active yeast
- 2/3 cup of warm water
- 2 cups of all-purpose flour
- 1 tsp. of salt
- 1, 10 ounce can of tomato sauce
- 1 pound of mozzarella cheese, shredded
- 12 cup of Romano cheese, grated
- ¼ cup of basil, chopped
- 1 Tbsp. of dried oregano
- 1 tsp. of crushed red pepper flakes
- 2 Tbsp. of extra virgin olive oil

Directions:

1. In a bowl, add in the water and active yeast. Stir well until the yeast dissolves.
2. Set aside to rest for 5 minutes or until foamy. Add in the all-purpose flour, dash of salt and olive oil. Stir well to mix.
3. Transfer the dough onto a greased surface. Knead the dough for 5 minutes. Transfer into a greased bowl. Cover and set aside to rest for 30 minutes.
4. Heat up the oven to 475 degrees. Transfer the dough onto a greased surface. Roll into a circle that is 12 inches in diameter. Transfer onto a pizza pan.
5. Spread the sauce over the pizza dough. Sprinkle the dried oregano, shredded mozzarella cheese, chopped basil, grated Romano cheese and crushed red pepper flakes over the top.
6. Place into the oven to bake for 10 to 15 minutes or until the crust is browned.

7. Remove and cool for 5 minutes before serving.

Nutrition:

Calorie: 250 kcal; Fat: 9 g; Carbs: 34 g; Sodium: 600 mg; Protein:12 g

48. Ham, Egg and Cheese Pizza

Preparation Time: 10 Minutes

Cooking Time: 15 Minutes

Servings: 4

Ingredients:

- 1 pound of pizza dough, store-bought
- 1 Tbsp. of extra virgin olive oil, extra for greasing
- 2 cups of mozzarella cheese, shredded
- 1 cup of ham, chopped
- 5 eggs
- Dash of black pepper
- Parsley, chopped and for garnish

Directions:

1. Heat up the oven to 425 degrees. Grease a pizza pan with olive oil. Roll the pizza dough onto the pizza pan.
2. Spread the remaining olive oil over the top of the crusts. Sprinkle the shredded mozzarella cheese and chopped ham over the top.
3. Crack the eggs directly over the top.
4. Season with a dash of black pepper. Place into the oven to bake for 15 minutes or until the eggs are set.
5. Remove and serve with a garnish of chopped parsley.

Nutrition:

Calorie: 204.1 kcal; Fat: 10.6 g; Carbs: 13.5 g; Sodium: 615.2 mg; Protein: 13.6 g

Chapter 6: Side Dishes and Vegetables

49.Sweet Potato And Pineapple Casserole

Preparation Time: 10 Minutes

Cooking Time: 20 Minutes

Servings: 6

Ingredients

- 1 (29 oz.) can sweet potatoes, drained
- 1 (8 oz.) can crushed pineapple, drained
- 1 tbsp. ground cinnamon
- 1/2 tsp. ground nutmeg
- 1/2 tsp. ground cloves
- 15 large marshmallows

Direction

1. Start preheating the oven to 350°F (175°C). Mash sweet potatoes in a big bowl until smooth.
2. Add cloves, nutmeg, cinnamon, and pineapple; stir thoroughly. Put in a 9x13-in. baking dish and put marshmallows on top.
3. Bake until the marshmallows turn golden, or about 20 minutes.

Nutrition

Calories: 208 kcal

Carbohydrate: 50.2 g

Fat: 0.5 g

Protein: 2.8 g

Sodium: 87 mg

50.Bacon And Almond Green Bean Casserole

Preparation Time: 10 Minutes

Cooking Time: 35 Minutes

Servings: 10

Ingredients

- 6 slices thick-cut bacon
- 1 1/2 cups whole milk
- 2 (10.75 oz.) cans condensed cream of mushroom soup
- 1/2 cup sliced almonds
- 3/4 tsp. garlic-pepper seasoning
- 3/4 (6 oz.) can French-fried onions
- 4 (14.5 oz.) cans green beans (such as Del Monte® Fresh Cut®), drained
- 1/4 (6 oz.) can French-fried onions

Direction

1. Start preheating the oven to 350°F (175°C). In a big frying pan, cook bacon over medium-high heat for 10 minutes until turning evenly brown, flipping sometimes.

2. Put on paper towels to strain, crumble into pieces, about 1 inch each. In a big bowl, combine cream of mushroom soup and milk together.

3. Add 3/4 can French-fried onion, garlic pepper, and almonds; toss to blend. Gently nestle green beans into the mixture. Add to a 9x9-in. glass or ceramic baking dish.

4. Put in the preheated oven and bake for 20 minutes until bubbling and fully cooked. Put the leftover 1/4 can French-fried onions on top; bake for 3-4 minutes until the onions turn light brown.

Nutrition

Calories:277 kcal; Carbohydrate:21g; Fat:18g; Protein:7g; Sodium:1139mg

51. Apple Stuffing Balls

Preparation Time: 15 Minutes; Cooking Time: 30 Minutes

Servings: 18

Ingredients

- 1/4 cup butter, cubed
- 1 large onion, finely chopped
- 2 celery ribs, finely chopped
- 3 large eggs, beaten
- 1/4 cup minced fresh parsley
- 3/4 tsp. salt
- 1/2 tsp. dried thyme
- 1/4 tsp. pepper
- 9 cups soft bread crumbs
- 2 medium apples, peeled and finely chopped

Direction

1. Set oven to 350° to preheat. Melt butter over medium heat in a large skillet. Sauté celery and onion in melted butter until just tender, about 4 to 6 minutes. Combine pepper, thyme, salt, parsley, and eggs in a large mixing bowl. Mix in onion mixture, apples, and bread crumbs.

2. Form the mixture in to balls of 2-inch in diameter. Line foil over the bottom of a 15x10x1-inch baking pan.

3. Arrange balls in the prepared baking pan.

4. Bake in the preheated oven until golden brown, about 30 to 35 minutes.

Nutrition

Calories: 106kcal; Carbohydrate: 14g; Fat: 4g; Protein: 3g; Sodium: 245mg

52.Jim's Veggie Casserole

Preparation Time: 10 Minutes

Cooking Time: 45 Minutes

Servings: 8

Ingredients

- 2 cups frozen green beans
- 1 (10.75 oz.) can cream of celery soup
- 1 cup sour cream
- 1 cup frozen shoepeg corn
- 1 (8 oz.) package shredded Cheddar cheese
- 1 (4 oz.) can sliced water chestnuts, drained
- 1 tsp. lemon juice
- Topping:
- 1 sleeve buttery round crackers (such as Ritz®), crushed
- ¼ cup butter, melted

Direction

1. Set oven to 350°F (175°C) to preheat. In a mixing bowl, combine lemon juice, water chestnuts, Cheddar cheese, shoepeg corn, sour cream, celery soup, and green beans; scatter to a casserole dish.
2. In a mixing bowl, combine crackers and butter; scatter over the top of the casserole.
3. Bake for about 45 minutes in the preheated oven until bubbly and hot.

Nutrition

Calories: 355 kcal; Carbohydrate: 18.5 g; Fat: 26.8 g; Protein: 10.2 g; Sodium: 659 mg

53. Cheesy Potato Casserole

Preparation Time: 15 Minutes

Cooking Time: 1 Hour

Servings: 12

Ingredients

- 1 lb. processed cheese
- 2 cups mayonnaise
- 1 (2 lb.) package frozen hash brown potatoes, thawed
- 1 white onion, chopped
- 1 (3 oz.) jar real bacon bits

Direction

1. Preheat oven to 350 °F (175 °C). Place the cheese in a large microwave-safe bowl, and microwave to melt. Stir in onions, potatoes and mayonnaise.
2. Spread in a baking dish of 9x13 inch and top with bacon bits.
3. In preheated oven, bake for about 1 hour or until bubbly and hot.

Nutrition

Calories: 476 kcal

Carbohydrate: 18.2 g

Fat: 44.8 g

Protein: 11.9 g

Sodium: 931 mg

54. Old Fashioned Potato Kugel

Preparation Time: 30 Minutes

Cooking Time: 1 Hour 30 Minutes

Servings: 24

Ingredients

- 1 tbsp. vegetable oil
- 10 potatoes, peeled and grated
- 2 onions, peeled and grated
- 5 eggs
- 1/3 cup vegetable oil
- 2 tsps. salt
- 1 tsp. black pepper

Direction

1. Set oven to 350°F (175°C) to preheat. Coat a 9x13-inch baking pan with 1 tbsp. vegetable oil.

2. In a large mixing bowl, combine onions and potatoes. Stir in pepper, salt, a third cup vegetable oil, and eggs.

3. Transfer mixture to the prepared baking pan. Bake for 1 1/2 to 2 hours in the 350°F (175°C) oven until top is crispy and golden brown.

Nutrition

Calories: 119 calories;

Carbohydrate: 16.5 g

Fat: 4.7 g

Protein: 3.2 g

Sodium: 214 mg

55.Baked Spinach

Preparation Time: 15 Minutes

Cooking Time: 1 Hour

Servings: 8

Ingredients

- 1 1/4 lbs. spinach
- 1/4 cup all-purpose flour
- 3 eggs, beaten
- 3/4 cup shredded Cheddar cheese
- 1/2 cup dried bread crumbs
- 2 tbsps. chopped fresh parsley (optional)
- 1/4 cup butter, melted
- 1 cup milk
- 1/2 tsp. salt
- 1/8 tsp. ground black pepper

Direction

1. Start preheating the oven to 350°F (175°C). Grease a 2-quart baking dish. Clean the spinach well.
2. Strain all excess liquid. Cut the spinach. Put flour and spinach in layers, fold beaten eggs approximately halfway between the layers. Stir together bread crumbs and cheese.
3. Stir in parsley if wanted. Sprinkle this mixture over the top of spinach. Stir together pepper, salt, milk, and margarine or butter.
4. Add to all of the ingredients. Bake for 50-60 minutes at 350°F (175°C) oven.

Nutrition

Calories: 193 kcal; Carbohydrate: 12.2 g; Fat: 12.4 g; Protein: 9.4 g

Sodium: 397 mg

56.Cheesy Zucchini Casserole

Preparation Time: 20 Minutes

Cooking Time: 1 Hour

Servings: 4

Ingredients

- 4 slices bread, cubed
- 1/4 cup melted butter
- 2 cups cubed zucchini
- 1 large onion, chopped
- 1 tsp. garlic salt
- 1 egg, beaten
- 2 cups shredded Cheddar cheese

Direction

1. Preheat oven to 350° F (175° C). In a medium bowl, add bread cubes then put melted butter on top of bread. Put in the egg, garlic salt, onion, and zucchini; properly mix.
2. Move into a 9x13-inch baking dish then cover with cheese. In the preheated oven, bake with cover for 30 minutes.
3. Remove cover and bake for 30 more minutes.

Nutrition

Calories: 437 kcal

Carbohydrate: 18.7 g

Fat: 32.4 g

Protein: 18.9 g

Sodium: 1076 mg

57.Cheesy Zucchini Rice Bake

Preparation Time: 10 Minutes

Cooking Time: 30 Minutes

Servings: 8

Ingredients

- 1 egg
- 1 cup milk
- 3 tbsps. margarine, melted
- 1 (10 oz.) can condensed cream of mushroom soup
- 2 cups cooked white rice
- 1 1/2 cups shredded zucchini
- 1 1/2 cups shredded Cheddar cheese, or more to taste

Direction

1. Preheat oven to 375° F (190° C). In a large bowl, beat the eggs. Pour into the egg the margarine and milk.
2. Gently pour the soup into the egg mixture, mixing to avoid lumps
3. . Whisk into mixture the Cheddar cheese, zucchini, and rice; transfer into an 8-inch baking dish.
4. In the preheated oven, bake for about 30 minutes till set.

Nutrition Information

Calories: 230 kcal ; Carbohydrate: 16.1 g ; Fat: 14.5 g; Protein: 9 g; Sodium: 431 mg

58. Granny's Squash Casserole

Preparation Time: 30 Minutes

Cooking Time: 45 Minutes

Servings: 15

Ingredients

- 2 lbs. yellow squash, chopped
- 1 onion, chopped
- 1 (10.75 oz.) can condensed cream of chicken soup
- 1 (8 oz.) container sour cream
- 4 tbsps. Butter
- 1 cup grated carrots
- 1 cup shredded Cheddar cheese
- 2 tbsps. Chopped pimento peppers
- salt and pepper to taste
- 1 (.7 oz.) package dry Italian-style salad dressing mix

Direction

1. Preheat an oven to 175°C/350°F.

2. Boil pot of salted water. Add onion and quash; cook till tender yet firm. Drain. Mix pepper, salt, pimento peppers, cheddar cheese, grated carrots, butter, sour cream, cream of chicken soup, onion and squash in big bowl.

3. Put mixture in medium baking dish; sprinkle Italian-style salad dressing mixture over.

4. Bake for 45 minutes at 175°C/350°F.

Nutrition Information

Calories: 194 kcal; Carbohydrate: 10.2 g; Fat: 15.1 g; Protein: 5.4 g

Sodium: 643 mg

59.Baked Sweet Potatoes

Preparation Time: 10 Minutes

Cooking Time: 1 Hour 5 Minutes

Servings: 4

Ingredients

- 2 tbsps. olive oil
- 3 large sweet potatoes
- 2 pinches dried oregano
- 2 pinches salt
- 2 pinches ground black pepper

Direction

1. Heat the oven beforehand to 175 °C or 350 °F. Use just enough olive oil to coat the bottom of a glass or non-stick baking dish.
2. Wash and peel the sweet potatoes then slice them into medium size pieces. Put them in the baking sheet and coat them with the olive oil by turning them.
3. Moderately sprinkle with pepper, salt and oregano to taste.
4. Bake in the preheated oven until soft, about 60 minutes.

Nutrition

Calories: 321 kcal; Carbohydrate: 61 g; Fat: 7.3 g; Protein: 4.8 g; Sodium: 92 mg

60.Pretzel Topped Sweet Potatoes

Preparation Time: 20 Minutes

Cooking Time: 25 Minutes

Servings: 12

Ingredients

- 13 pretzel rods, crushed
- 1 cup chopped pecans
- 1 cup fresh cranberries
- 1 cup packed light brown sugar
- 1 cup melted butter, divided
- 1 (32 oz.) can sweet potatoes, drained
- 1 (5 oz.) can evaporated milk
- 1/2 cup white sugar
- 1 tsp. vanilla extract

Direction

1. Start preheating the oven to 350°F (175°C). Oil a 9x13-in. baking dish. In a bowl, mix together 1/2 cup melted butter, brown sugar, cranberries, pecans, and pretzels. In a bowl, whisk sweet potatoes together until smooth
2. Add the leftover 1/2 cup melted butter, vanilla extract, sugar, and evaporated milk and stir until smooth.
3. Ladle the mixture into the prepared baking dish, sprinkle over the top with the pretzel mixture.
4. Put in the preheated oven and bake for 25-30 minutes until the edges are bubbly.

Nutrition Information

Calories: 428 kcal ; Carbohydrate: 53.5 g; Fat: 23.3 g; Protein: 4.2 g; Sodium: 387 mg

Chapter 7: Easy Dinner Recipe for One

61. Pork Chops with Balsamic Roasted Vegetables

Preparation Time: 5 Minutes

Cooking Time: 30 Minutes

Servings: **2**

Ingredients:

- 2 pork chops
- 6 oz small red potatoes, halved
- 4 oz cremini mushrooms, halved
- 2-3 carrots, cut into sticks
- 1 medium red onion, cut into wedges
- ½ tsp thyme
- ½ tsp. ground cumin
- 2 tbsps. olive oil
- ½ tsp tomato paste
- ¼ cup chicken broth
- ½ tbsp honey
- 2 tbsp balsamic vinegar
- ¼ cup Gorgonzola cheese, crumbled
- salt and black pepper, to taste

Directions:

1. Heat olive oil in an ovenproof casserole and cook pork chops 3 minutes on each side or until browned.
2. Add the potatoes, carrots, onion and mushrooms. Season with salt and pepper, sprinkle with thyme and cumin.
3. In a bowl, combine tomato paste, balsamic vinegar, honey and chicken broth. Pour this mixture over the pork chops and vegetables.
4. Cover and bake in a preheated to 420 F on for 30 minutes, stirring halfway through.

Nutrition:

Calorie: 385 kcal

Fat: 21.7 g

Carbs: 21 g

Sodium: 415 mg

Protein: 27 g

62.Juicy Pork Chops

Preparation Time: 5 Minutes

Cooking Time: 45 Minutes

Servings: 2

Ingredients:

- 2 garlic cloves, crushed
- ½ tbsp. Honey
- 2 tbsps. olive oil
- ½ tbsp vinegar
- ½ cup white wine
- ½ tbsp soy sauce
- ½ tbsp ketchup
- ¼ tsp dried sage
- ½ tsp black pepper
- ¼ tsp salt
- 2-3 pork chops, about 4 oz each

Directions:

1. In a cup, combine all liquid ingredients and stir until very well mixed.

2. Crush the garlic, sage, black pepper and salt together into a paste. Rub each chop with the garlic paste and arrange them in a casserole dish. Pour the liquid mix over the chops.

3. Cover the casserole and bake in a preheated to 350 F on for 45 minutes, or until the chops are cooked through.

Nutrition:

Calorie: 322 kcal; Fat: 17.3 g; Carbs: 0.1 g; Sodium: 248.6 mg; Protein: 39.0 g

63. Pork with Orange and Olives

Preparation Time: 5 Minutes

Cooking Time: 45 Minutes

Servings: 2

Ingredients:

- 1 lb. pork shoulder, cut into cubes
- 1 lb. potatoes, peeled and cut into large wedges
- 1 onion, chopped
- 2-3 garlic cloves, chopped
- 1 can tomatoes, undrained
- 1/2 cup sun-dried tomatoes
- 1 cup black olives, halved
- 3 bay leaves
- 3 tbsp olive oil
- ¼ cup orange juice
- ¼ cup white wine
- ½ tsp paprika
- ½ tsp orange zest
- ½ tsp black pepper
- ¼ tsp salt

Directions:

1. Heat olive in an ovenproof casserole and seal pork until golden. Stir in onions, garlic, paprika, orange zest, wine and orange juice.

2. Add potatoes, bay leaves, olives, sun-dried tomatoes and canned tomatoes. Stir to combine.

3. Cover the casserole and bake in a preheated to 350 F on for 45 minutes, or until the chops are cooked through.

4. Uncover and cook until the liquid evaporates.

Nutrition:

Calorie: 210 kcal

Fat: 12 g

Carbs: 6 g

Sodium: 590 mg

Protein: 22 g

64.Shrimp-Asparagus Roast

Preparation Time: 5 minutes

Cooking Time: 15–20 minutes

Serving: 3–4

Ingredients

- ¼ cup parmesan cheese, grated

For asparagus

- 1-pound asparagus, woody ends trimmed off
- 2 tablespoons olive oil
- Salt and pepper, to taste

For shrimp

- 1-pound raw shrimp, shelled
- 1 tablespoon olive oil
- Zest of one lemon
- 1–2 teaspoons red pepper flakes, or to taste
- Salt and pepper, to taste

Directions

1. Preheat oven to 425°F. Line and grease a sheet pan. In a bowl, combine ingredients for shrimp.
2. Set aside Lay asparagus on a baking sheet and drizzle or brush with olive oil. Season with salt and pepper.
3. Place in oven and let bake for 10 to 15 minutes. Place the shrimp in the sheet pan with the asparagus. Cook until shrimp are pink and opaque (about 5 minutes).
4. Sprinkle with grated parmesan and serve.

Nutrition

Calories 280 kcal; Carbs 9.4 g ; Fat 10 g; Protein 38.4 g; Sodium 836 mg

65.Roasted Salmon with Lemon & Rosemary

Preparation Time: 5 minutes; Cooking Time: 20 minutes

Serving: 2

Ingredients

- 2 6-ounce salmon fillets, skinless and boneless
- ½ pound vegetables of choice (like asparagus, green beans, bok choy or thinly sliced zucchini)
- 1 lemon, sliced thinly and divided
- 3 sprigs fresh rosemary, divided
- Salt and pepper, to taste
- 1-2 tablespoons olive oil, divided

Directions

1. Preheat oven to 400°F. Line and grease a sheet pan.
2. Layer the vegetables, half the lemon slices and half the rosemary on the sheet pan, in that order, drizzling each layer with about a tablespoon of olive oil. Place the salmon fillets over the sprigs of rosemary.
3. Season with salt and pepper. Arrange the remaining rosemary sprigs over the fish. Top with remaining lemon slices and drizzle with remaining olive oil.
4. Bake until fish can be flaked easily with a fork and vegetables are tender (about 20 minutes).

Nutrition

Calories 257 kcal; Carbs 6 g ; Fat 18 g ; Protein 20.5 g ; Sodium 1017 mg

66.Salmon and Green Bean Packets

Preparation Time: 15 minutes

Cooking Time: 25 minutes

Serving: 3

Ingredients

- 3 6-ounce salmon fillets
- ½ pound French beans, washed
- ½ lemon, sliced thinly

Ranch seasoning

- 1 teaspoon dried parsley
- ½ teaspoon garlic powder
- ½ teaspoon onion powder
- ¼ teaspoon salt
- ¼ teaspoon dried chives
- ¼ teaspoon dried dill
- ¼ teaspoon ground black pepper

Directions

1. Preheat oven to 400°F. In a small bowl or Ziploc bag, combine ranch seasoning ingredients.

2. Prepare a sheet of foil large enough to contain some beans and a fillet, with extra to fold over and seal to form a packet. Arrange some beans in a single layer at the center of the foil sheet.

3. Sprinkle with ranch seasoning. Place a salmon fillet on the beans and season well. Place slices of lemon on top. Fold the edges over and seal into a packet.

4. Repeat with the rest of the fish, beans, and lemon slices, to make six packets. Place onto baking sheets and cook until fish is just flaky but moist and beans are tender (about 25 minutes).

Nutrition

Calories 480; Carbs 27.9 g; Fat 21.9 g; Protein 42.6 g; Sodium 284 mg

67.Salmon & Sweet Potato

Preparation Time: 5 minutes

Cooking Time: 30 minutes

Serving: 3

Ingredients

- 3 6-ounce salmon fillets
- 4–5 cups asparagus, woody ends trimmed off, or zucchini, sliced thinly
- 1 large sweet potato, peeled & cubed
- 2 tablespoons olive oil
- ½ teaspoon garlic powder
- ½ teaspoon thyme
- Salt & pepper to taste

Directions

1. Preheat oven to 350°F. Line and grease a sheet pan. Arrange the salmon fillets at the center of the pan and surround with the vegetables.

2. Drizzle or brush with olive oil. Season with garlic powder, thyme, salt and pepper.

3. Bake until salmon flakes easily and vegetables are tender (about 30 minutes).

Nutrition

Calories 495 ; Carbs 19.4 g ; Fat 30.4 g ; Protein 38 g ; Sodium 490 mg

68.Lemon-Garlic Shrimp with Brussels Sprouts

Preparation Time: 5 minutes plus 20 minutes marinating time

Cooking Time: 20 minutes

Serves: 2

Ingredients

- 1-pound shrimp, cleaned, peeled & deveined
- 3 cups Brussels sprouts, cleaned & sliced in half
- 2 tablespoons olive oil
- ½ teaspoon garlic powder
- Salt & pepper, to taste
- 1 lemon, cut into wedges

Marinade for shrimp

- 2 tablespoons lemon juice
- 2 tablespoons olive oil
- 6 cloves garlic, minced
- 1 teaspoon dried parsley
- 1 teaspoon dried basil
- ½ teaspoon red pepper flakes
- Salt & pepper, to taste

Directions

1. Combine marinade ingredients in a bowl or Ziploc bag. Add shrimp and coat well.

2. Let marinate for 20 minutes. Preheat oven to 350°F. Line and grease a sheet pan. Place the Brussels sprouts on the sheet pan, brush with olive oil and season with garlic powder, salt and pepper.

3. Bake for 10 minutes. Remove sheet from and add the marinated shrimp in the center of the sheet pan and surrounded with Brussels sprouts.

4. Bake until shrimp are pink and opaque (about 20 minutes).

5. Serve with lemon wedges, if desired.

Nutrition

Calories 227

Carbs 9.4 g

Fat 10.3 g

Protein 28 g

Sodium 696 mg

69.Chicken with Herb Sauce

Preparation Time: 10 minutes

Cooking Time: 35–45 minutes

Serving: 2

Ingredients

- 2 chicken breasts or thighs, bone-in and skin-on
- 2-3 cups vegetables of choice

For herb sauce

- 1/8 cup olive oil
- 1 tablespoon dry parsley, chopped
- ½ small onion, minced
- 1 cloves garlic, minced
- ½ teaspoon dried thyme
- ¼ teaspoon dry rosemary
- ¼ teaspoon dry marjoram
- Juice of 1 lemon
- 1/8 teaspoon hot sauce, or to taste (optional)
- Salt and pepper, to taste

Directions

1. Preheat oven to 425°F. Line and grease a sheet pan. Place the chicken in the middle of the sheet pan, skin side up, in a single layer. Place vegetables around the chicken.

2. Combine sauce ingredients and drizzle over chicken and vegetables. Bake until chicken is cooked through and vegetables are tender (about 35–45 minutes).

3. If desired, transfer sheet pan to top rack and broil to make brown and crisp (about 2–5 minutes).

Nutrition

Calories 721

Carbs 50.9 g

Fat 27.2 g

Protein 66.5 g

Sodium 504 mg

Note: if using peas, place them on the sheet pan, just a few minutes, about 5-8 minutes before the chicken is done.

70. Easy Sausage & Veggie Dinner

Preparation Time: 5 minutes

Cooking Time: 30–40 minutes

Serves: 2

Ingredients

- 1 tablespoons olive oil
- ½ teaspoon garlic powder
- ¼ teaspoon salt, or to taste
- 1/8 teaspoon freshly-ground black pepper
- 3-4 large pork sausages, cut into chunks
- 1 medium onions, each cut into 6–8 wedges
- 1-pound vegetables of choice (like broccoli florets, cherry tomatoes, carrot chunks, diced sweet potato, trimmed green beans or asparagus, potato wedges, Brussels sprout wedges, etc.)

Directions

1. Preheat oven to 400°F. Line and grease a sheet pan.
2. Place vegetables, including onions, in sheet pan, spreading into a single layer.
3. Brush with oil and season with garlic powder, salt and pepper.
4. Place sausages between vegetables.
5. Bake until internal temperature of sausages reaches 165°F (about 30–40 minutes). The surface will begin to brown and the contents will sizzle. Flip over halfway through cooking for even browning. If needed, remove vegetables to prevent overcooking and continue cooking sausages.

Nutrition

Calories 205; Carbs17.5 g; Fat 12.4 g; Protein 10.0 g; Sodium 493 mg

71.Stuffed Peppers with Taco Seasoning

Preparation Time: 20 minutes

Cooking Time: 25–30 minutes

Serving: 4

Ingredients

- 4 medium red or green bell peppers, stemmed, seeded and halved lengthwise
- 1 tablespoon olive oil
- Salt and pepper, to taste
- 1–2 limes, cut into wedges

For filling

- 1 tablespoon olive oil
- 4 cloves garlic, minced
- 1-pound lean ground beef
- ½ small onion, minced

For topping

- ¼ cup sour cream
- ¼ cup shredded cheddar or Monterey Jack cheese
- 1 medium tomato, diced
- 1 teaspoon chili powder, or to taste

- ½ teaspoon salt
- ½ teaspoon cumin
- ¼ teaspoon oregano
- ⅛ teaspoon paprika
- ⅛ teaspoon black pepper
- 1 15½-ounce can kidney beans, drained and rinsed
- 1 8-ounce can tomato sauce

Directions

Preheat oven to 350°F. Arrange bell pepper halves on sheet pan and brush with olive oil. Season lightly with salt and pepper.

Prepare filling. Heat oil in a large skillet over medium heat. Add the garlic, onion and beef. Cook, stirring frequently, until meat is no longer pink. Stir in the rest of the filling ingredients and bring to a boil.

Reduce heat and let simmer for 5 minutes. Stuff peppers with filling. Pour enough water into sheet pan to fill the bottom.

Bake until peppers are tender and slightly browned (about 15–20 minutes). Add a little more water to the pan, if needed.

It should dry out when the peppers are done.

Top each stuffed pepper with cheese, tomato and cream. Serve with lime wedges.

Nutrition

Calories 680

Carbs 77 g

Fat 19 g

Protein 52 g

Sodium 1850 mg

Chapter 8: Easy Dinner Recipe for Whole Family

72. Tuna Pasta Casserole

Preparation Time: 30 Minutes

Cooking Time: 30 Minutes

Servings: 4

Ingredients:

- 1 cup onion, chopped
- 2 cups mushrooms, sliced
- 3 oz. noodles
- 1 cup stir-fry vegetables
- 1 cup broccoli florets
- ¾ cup low-fat milk
- 11 oz. low-fat mushroom soup
- Salt to taste
- 1/2 teaspoon dried dill
- 6 oz. tuna flakes
- 2 tablespoons Parmesan cheese, grated

Directions

1. Preheat your oven to 375 degrees F. In pan over medium heat, cook the onion, mushrooms, noodles, stir-fry veggies and broccoli in hot water for 3 minutes.
2. Drain and set aside. In a bowl, mix the milk, cream of mushroom, salt and dill. Add to the noodles. Stir in the tuna flakes.
3. Transfer the mixture to a baking pan. Bake for 25 minutes.
4. Sprinkle the Parmesan cheese on top. Bake for another 5 minutes.

Nutrition

Calories 222 kcal

Fat 4 g

Carbohydrates 27.5 g

Protein 18.2 g

Sodium 685 mg

73.Sausage Sweet Potato Casserole

Preparation Time: 20 Minutes

Cooking Time: 1 Hour

Servings: 8

Ingredients:

- Cooking spray
- 6 oz. turkey sausage
- 1 cup onion, chopped
- 4 cloves garlic, crushed and minced
- 1 cup red sweet pepper, chopped
- 1 tablespoon water
- 1 teaspoon olive oil
- 5 oz. baby spinach
- 1 ½ cups sweet potatoes, roasted
- 8 eggs, beaten
- 4 egg whites
- ½ cup nonfat milk
- ½ teaspoon dry mustard
- ½ teaspoon red pepper flakes
- Salt and pepper to taste
- 2 tablespoons green onion, chopped
- 2 oz. goat cheese, crumbled

Directions

1. Preheat your oven to 350 degrees F. Spray your baking pan with oil. In pan over medium heat, cook the sausage for 6 minutes, stirring frequently.
2. Drain the fat. In the same pan, add the garlic, onion and sweet pepper. Cook for 7 minutes.
3. Pour in the water. Scrape the browned bits using a wooden spoon. Stir in the spinach and cook for 2 minutes. Add the sweet potatoes and sausage. Mix well. Transfer the mixture to a baking pan. In a bowl, beat eggs and egg whites.
4. Stir in the milk and season with the mustard, red pepper flakes, salt and pepper. Pour this mixture over the sausages.
5. Bake in the oven for 40 minutes. Sprinkle with the green onion and goat cheese before serving.

Nutrition

Calories 219 kcal

Fat 11.4 g

Carbohydrates 11.9 g

Protein 17 g

Sodium 446 mg

74.Healthy Salmon & Veggies

Preparation Time: 10 minutes

Cooking Time: 30 minutes

Serving: 2

Ingredients:

- 1-pound Asparagus
- 2 tsps. Fresh dill
- 2 cups Baby potatoes
- 1 tablespoon Extra virgin olive oil
- 10 oz. Salmon
- ⅛ teaspoon Salt
- 2 Lemon wedges
- 1/8 teaspoon Garlic powder

Directions:

1. Prepare the oven by preheating to 450ºF.
2. Now proceed to line a sheet pan with parchment paper and set aside. Slice the potatoes in half from the top and throw them in a mixing bowl. Drizzle olive oil over it and toss to mix. Sprinkle garlic powder and salt. Toss again. Pour potatoes onto the sheet pan and spread them out so they bake evenly.
3. Slide the pan into the oven and bake for about 20 minutes. Meanwhile, you have some free time on your hands so why not chop the dill and trim the asparagus.
4. Place the salmon with the skin down on another sheet pan and sprinkle dill, pepper and salt over it. Place asparagus right beside seasoned salmon and bake for roughly 10 minutes.
5. Drizzle lemon juice over the salmon and serve with baked potatoes.

Nutrition:

Calorie: 500 kcal; Fat: 14.1 g; Carbs: 26.1 g; Fiber: 5.0 g; Protein: 30.9 g

75.Juicy Oven-Baked Cajun Chicken Breasts

Preparation Time: 10 minutes

Cooking Time: 20 minutes

Serving: 4

Ingredients:

- 1 tsp. Ground garlic
- 1 tsp. Dried thyme powder
- 1 tsp. Onion powder
- ½ tsp. Cayenne pepper
- 2-pounds Skinned chicken breast
- 2 tsps. Paprika
- 1 tsp. Dried oregano
- 4 tbsps. Extra virgin olive oil
- 1 tsp. Salt
- 1 tsp. Black pepper powder
- Cooking spray

Directions

1. Set your oven to 425°F. Prepare a sheet pan, line it with aluminum foil and coat the foil with cooking spray.
2. Get a mixing bowl. Pour in garlic powder, paprika, black pepper, onion powder, dried oregano, salt, dried thyme and cayenne pepper. Mix thoroughly.

3. Use the spice mixture above to coat the chicken breasts before spreading then out on the lined sheet pan. Drizzle some olive oil on top of the chicken breasts and slide the pan into the oven to bake. Let them bake for about 20 minutes.
4. Take the sheet pan out of the oven and allow it to cool for 5 minutes. Serve warm.

Nutrition:

Calorie: 310 kcal; Fat: 0.2 g; Carbs: 33.6 g; Fiber 2.3 g; Protein: 3.2 g

76.Sheet Pan Shrimp Boil

Preparation Time: 5 minutes

Cooking Time: 27 minutes

Serving: 4

Ingredients:

- ¼ cup melted unsalted butter
- 1 tbsp. old bay seasoning
- 1 medium size lemon wedges
- 1-pound Baby Dutch yellow potatoes
- 4 cloves minced garlic
- 2 tbsps. freshly chopped parsley
- 1 package sliced smoked andouille sausage
- 1-pound peeled veinless shrimp
- 6 pieces cut corn ears

Directions:

1. First things first, set your oven to 400°F. Lightly grease a sheet pan with nonstick vegetable oil cooking spray.
2. Set aside. Put a pot of salted water over medium heat and pour in washed potatoes. Let it cook for 13 minutes or until it's a bit tender. Add the corn 5 minutes to the end of cooking then drain excess water. Mix garlic, old bay seasoning and butter in a tiny bowl.
3. Pour shrimp, potatoes, sausages and corn onto the sheet pan and spread them out. Scoop butter mixture onto the pan and toss gently so you don't break up the potatoes.
4. Make sure everything is coated is coated in butter mixture before you slide sheet pan into the oven to bake.
5. Leave to bake for 15 minutes or more if the corn isn't tender enough or the shrimp doesn't look opaque.
6. Serve warm with parsley toppings and lemon wedges.

Nutrition:

Calorie: 30 kcal; Fat: 2.5 g; Carbs: 2 g; Fiber: 5g; Protein: 1 g

77.Parmesan Crusted Tilapia with Mayo

Preparation Time: 5 minutes

Cooking Time: 10 minutes

Serving: 6

Ingredients:

- 1 ½ tsp. garlic salt
- 6 tbsps. shredded parmesan cheese
- 6.5-ouces Tilapia fillets
- ½ tsp. black pepper powder This is optional.
- Lemon. This is optional.
- ¼ cup mayonnaise
- Soft low carb vegetables (ex. green beans, tomatoes, zucchini, etc.). This is optional.

Directions:

1. Prepare your oven, set it to 400°F.
2. Prepare your sheet pan too. Line it with parchment paper or aluminum foil and spray either one with cooking spray.
3. Arrange the tilapia fillets on the sheet pan and season with black pepper and garlic salt. Flip and do the same to the other side.

4. Glaze each fillet with 2 teaspoons on mayonnaise and layer shredded parmesan cheese on top. You can choose to place some soft low carb vegetables like bell peppers around the fillets in an even layer.
5. Harder veggies won't work because the fish won't really give them time to cook through. Pour olive oil, salt and pepper over them and put the pan in the oven to cook.
6. The cooking time depends on the fish, so you see why we used soft vegetables. 12 to 15 minutes tops.
7. Drizzle lemon juice over it and serve.

Nutrition:

Calorie: 186 kcal; Fat: 14 g; Carbs: 0.2 g; Fiber: 0.1 g; Protein: 15 g

78. Maple-Glazed Salmon with Apples and Fennel

Preparation Time: 10

Cooking Time: 12

Servings: 4

Ingredients:

- ¼ cup whole-grain mustard
- ¼ cup Grade-A pure maple syrup
- 2 tablespoons olive oil
- 2 pounds salmon fillets
- 2 large fennel bulbs, root ends and green stalks trimmed, bulb cut into strips
- 2 green apples, peeled, cored, and sliced

Directions:

1. Preheat the oven to 450°F.
2. Line a sheet pan with aluminum foil. In a small bowl, thoroughly whisk the mustard, maple syrup, and olive oil. Set aside.
3. Arrange the salmon on one side of the sheet pan. In a medium bowl, toss together the fennel and apples.
4. Transfer to the other end of the sheet pan. Brush the salmon fillets with the maple glaze and drizzle any remaining glaze on the apples and fennel.
5. Bake for 10 to 12 minutes, or until the salmon is cooked and registers an internal temperature of 165°F on a meat thermometer.

Nutrition:

Calories: 554 kcal; Fat: 28g; Sodium: 356mg; Carbs: 38g; Protein: 40g

79.Sweet Chili and Lime Shrimp with Sugar Snap Peas

Preparation Time: 20 Minutes

Cooking Time: 8 Minutes

Servings: 4

Ingredients

- ⅓ cup orange marmalade
- ¼ cup soy sauce
- ¼ cup freshly squeezed lime juice
- 2 tablespoons olive oil
- 1 teaspoon ground ginger
- 2 teaspoons chili garlic paste
- 2 pounds fresh shrimp, or frozen and thawed, rinsed, shells removed including tails
- 1-pound sugar snap peas, strings removed

Directions

1. Preheat the oven to 400°F. Line a sheet pan with aluminum foil. Set aside. In a large bowl, stir together the marmalade, soy sauce, lime juice, chili garlic paste, and ginger.

2. Add the shrimp and toss to coat. Arrange the sugar snap peas on one side of the prepared sheet pan and drizzle with the olive oil. Add the shrimp to the other side of the pan, scraping out any remaining sauce onto the shrimp.

3. Bake for 5 to 8 minutes, or until all of the shrimp have cooked and are completely pink inside.

Nutrition:

Calories: 413 kcal; Fat: 10 g; Sodium: 1447 mg; Carbs: 30 g, Protein: 52g

80.Classic Garlic-Baked Chicken Thighs

Preparation Time: 10 minutes

Cooking Time: 20 minutes

Serving: 4

Ingredients:

- 4 tsp. Pepper
- ½ tsp Garlic powder
- ½ tsp Salt
- 2 tbsp. Extra virgin olive oil
- 4 large size Chicken thighs
- Vegetable oil cooking spray

Directions:

1. Prepare oven by preheating to 425°F. Get a sheet pan lined with aluminum spoil and then coated with cooking spray.
2. In a mixing bowl, add pepper, garlic powder, olive oil and salt. Mix thoroughly. Throw the chicken into the bowl and toss until it is completely coated in the flavored olive oil.
3. Arrange seasoned chicken thighs on the sheet pan making sure to spread them out for even cooking.
4. Slide the pan into the oven and roast for about 20 minutes or more if the chicken isn't cooked through.
5. Take the pan out of the oven and let it sit for 5 minutes. Serve warm.

Nutrition:

Calorie: 550 kcal; Fat: 48 g; Carbs: 0 g; Fiber: 0 g; Protein: 40 g

Sheet Pan Steak And Veggies

Prep time: 15 minutes Cooking time: 15 minutes

Serving: 6

Ingredients:

- 3 cloves Minced garlic
- 2 pounds Baby red potatoes
- 1 tsp. Dried thyme
- 2 pounds Dry top sirloin steak
- 2 tbsp. Extra virgin olive oil
- Kosher salt
- 16 oz Broccoli florets
- Black pepper powder

Directions:

1. Set oven to 350°F. Grease a sheet pan with a bit of cooking spray. Set a pot of water on medium heat, add salt and potatoes. Cook for 15 minutes so it becomes parboiled. Now drain it and set aside.
2. Arrange broccoli on the greased sheet pan in an even layer. Season with salt, garlic, pepper and thyme. Drizzle a bit of olive oil over that and gently toss to coat. You want everything properly seasoned. Sprinkle salt and pepper over the steaks to season them. Place them on the same sheet pan in an even layer and slide pan into the oven to bake.
3. This should bake until the meat is browned and slightly burnt at the edges. If you enjoy medium rare, let it cook for only 5 minutes before you flip to the other side so 10 minutes in total.
4. Take out of oven and serve warm. Top with garlic butter if you like

Nutrition:

Calorie: 480 kcal; Fat: 24 g; Carbs: 30 g; Fiber: 5 g; Protein: 36 g

Table of Contents

Chapter 9: Dessert

81.Yummy Chocolate Cake

Preparation Time: 20 Minutes

Cooking Time: 35 Minutes

Servings: 16

Ingredients:

- 1 package chocolate cake mix
- 1-3/4 cups water
- 3 egg whites
- 1 package (2.1 oz.) sugar-free instant chocolate pudding mix

Frosting:

- 1-1/4 cups cold fat-free milk
- ¼ tsp. almond extract
- 1 package (1.4 oz.) sugar-free instant chocolate pudding mix
- 1 carton (8 oz.) frozen reduced-fat whipped topping, thawed

Directions:

1. Blend egg whites, water, pudding mix and cake mix together in a big bowl. Beat for 60 seconds over low speed, then switch to medium speed and beat for 2 minutes.
2. Transfer to a 15x10x1-inch baking pan greased with cooking spray. Bake at 350 degrees until a toothpick slid into the middle comes out with no streaks of batter, about 12 to 18 minutes. Allow to cool on a wire rack. Put extract and milk into a big bowl to make frosting. Scatter in 1/3 of the pudding mix and allow to stand for 60 seconds. Stir pudding into milk.
3. Do the same thing two times with the rest of pudding mix. Stir pudding for another 2 minutes. Allow to sit for 15 minutes.

4. Fold whipped topping into the mixture. Frost the cake. If preferred, add on chocolate curls to decorate.

Nutrition:

Calories: 197kcal; Carbohydrate: 35g; Fat: 5g; Protein: 3g; Sodium: 409mg

82.Raspberry Swirl Cheesecake Pie

Preparation Time: 20 Minutes

Cooking Time: 45 Minutes

Servings: 6-8

Ingredients

- Pastry for single-crust pie (9 inches)
- 2 packages (8 oz. each) cream cheese, softened
- 1/2 cup sugar
- 1/2 tsp. vanilla extract
- 2 eggs
- 3 tbsps. raspberry jam

Direction

1. Use heavy-duty foil with double thickness to line unpricked pastry shell. Bake for 5 minutes at 450°; take away the foil. Bake for another 5 minutes. Take out of the oven, lower the temperature to 350°.
2. Whisk vanilla, sugar, and cream cheese together in a bowl. Add eggs, whisking on low speed until just blended. Add to the pastry shell. Whisk jam, drizzle the jam over the filling.
3. Swirl the jam by slicing through the filling with a knife. Bake until the middle has nearly set, about 25-30 minutes. Put on a wire rack to cool, about 60 minutes. Chill overnight.
4. Allow to sit at room temperature before cutting, about 30 minutes.

Nutrition:

Calories: 305 calories; Carbohydrate: 31 g; Fat: 18 g; Protein: 5 g; Sodium: 200 mg

83.Cherry Cheese Delight

Preparation Time: 20 Minutes

Cooking Time: 40 Minutes

Servings: 12-15

Ingredients:

- 1 cup all-purpose flour
- 1 cup chopped pecans
- 1/2 cup packed brown sugar
- 1/2 cup butter, softened

Filling:

- 2 packages (8 oz. each) cream cheese, softened
- 1/2 cup confectioners' sugar
- 1 tsp. vanilla extract
- 1 carton (12 oz.) frozen whipped topping, thawed
- 2 cans (21 oz. each) cherry pie filling

Directions:

1. Mix the brown sugar, pecans and flour in a small bowl. Mix in the butter till crumbly. Pat lightly into a 13x9-inch ungreased baking dish. Bake for 18 to 20 minutes at 350°, until golden brown. Cool entirely.
2. Beat the vanilla, confectioner's sugar and cream cheese until smooth in a large bowl for the filling.
3. Fold in the whipped topping. Spread the filling over the crust carefully. Add pie filling on top.
4. Cover then refrigerate for minimum of 2 hours.

Nutrition:

Calories: 344kcal; Carbohydrate: 35g; Fat:21g; Protein:3g; Sodium: 117mg

84. White Chocolate Torte

Preparation Time: 20 Minutes

Cooking Time: 45 Minutes

Servings: 14-16

Ingredients:

- 1 cup butter, softened
- 2 cups sugar
- 4 oz. white baking chocolate, melted and cooled
- 4 large eggs
- 1-1/2 tsps. clear vanilla extract
- 3 cups all-purpose flour
- 1 tsp. baking soda
- 1 cup buttermilk
- 1/2 cup water
- 1/2 cup chopped pecans, toasted

Frosting:

- 11 oz. cream cheese, softened
- 1/3 cup butter, softened
- 4 oz. white baking chocolate, melted and cooled
- 1-1/2 tsps. clear vanilla extract
- 6-1/2 cups confectioners' sugar
- Chocolate curls

Directions:

1. Line waxed paper on 3 9-in. greased round baking pans; grease paper. Put aside. Cream sugar and butter till fluffy and light in big bowl; beat chocolate in.

2. One by one, add eggs; beat well with every addition. Beat vanilla in. Mix baking soda and flour; alternately with water and buttermilk, add to creamed mixture slowly.

3. Beat well with every addition. Fold pecans in; put batter in prepped pans.

4. Bake for 23-27 minutes at 350° or till inserted toothpick in middle exits clean; cool for 10 minutes.

5. Transfer from pans onto wire racks. Throw waxed paper.

Frosting: Beat butter and cream cheese till fluffy in big bowl; beat vanilla and chocolate in. Add confectioners' sugar slowly till smooth; spread frosting on top, sides and between layers of cake. Garnish using chocolate curls; keep in fridge.

Nutrition:

Calories: 885 calories; Carbohydrate: 103 g; Fat: 49 g; Protein: 11 g; Sodium: 491 mg

85. Raspberry Supreme Cheesecake

Preparation Time: 25 Minutes

Cooking Time: 25 Minutes

Servings: 16-20 servings.

Ingredients

- 2 cups graham cracker crumbs
- 1 cup chopped toasted almonds
- 1/2 cup sugar
- 2/3 cup butter, melted
- 1 package (8 oz.) cream cheese, softened
- 1 can (14 oz.) sweetened condensed milk
- 1/3 cup lemon juice
- 1 tsp. vanilla extract
- 1 package (6 oz.) raspberry gelatin
- 2 cups hot water
- 2 packages (10 oz. each) frozen raspberries, partially thawed
- 2 cups whipped cream
- 1/4 cup toasted slivered almonds

Direction

1. Mix the first 4 ingredients. Press into a 13x9-inch dish; chill for half an hour. In the meantime, whisk vanilla, lemon juice, milk, and cream cheese until smooth. Pour over the crust; chill.
2. Dissolve the gelatin in the water. Add the raspberries, stir until they are thawed completely; chill until they become very thick.
3. Pour over the fillings. Chill until set. Add almonds and whipped cream on top before serving. Chill in the fridge.

Nutrition:

Calories:313kcal; Carbohydrate:43g; Fat: 14g; Protein: 5g; Sodium: 178mg

86.Zucchini Chip Cupcakes

Preparation Time: 15m ; Cooking Time: 35m

Servings: 2 dozen

Ingredients:

- 1/2 cup butter, softened
- 1/2 cup canola oil
- 1-3/4 cups sugar
- 2 eggs
- 1/2 cup milk
- 1 tsp. vanilla extract
- 2-1/2 cups all-purpose flour
- 1/4 cup baking cocoa
- 1 tsp. baking soda
- 1/2 tsp. salt
- 1/2 tsp. ground cinnamon
- 2 cups shredded zucchini
- 1/4 cup miniature semisweet chocolate chips
- 1/4 cup chopped pecans

Directions:

1. Cream sugar, oil, and butter in a large bowl until they are fluffy and light. Whisk in vanilla, milk, and eggs.
2. Mix cinnamon, salt, baking soda, cocoa, and flour; add into the creamed mixture gradually Fold in chocolate chips and zucchini.
3. Add into paper-lined or greased muffin cups to 2/3 full. Place pecans on top. Bake at 375 degrees until a toothpick comes out clean, for 20-25 minutes.
4. Let cool for 10 minutes, then transfer from the pans onto wire racks to cool entirely

Nutrition:

Calories:208kcal; Carbohydrate:27g; Fat: 11g; Protein: 3g; Sodium: 149mg

87.Cinnamon Cupcakes

Preparation Time: 25 Minutes

Cooking Time: 45 Minutes

Servings: 18

Ingredients:

- 3/4 cup butter, softened
- 1-1/4 cups sugar
- 4 large egg whites
- 1 tsp. vanilla extract
- 2-1/4 cups cake flour
- 2 tsps. baking powder
- 1/2 tsp. salt

CINNAMON FROSTING:

- 1/4 cup butter, softened
- 1 tsp. clear vanilla extract
- 1/4 tsp. ground cinnamon
- 2-1/4 cups confectioners' sugar
- 3 tbsps. 2% milk
- Additional ground cinnamon
- 3/4 cup 2% milk
- Topping:
- 2 tbsps. sugar
- 1/2 tsp. ground cinnamon

Directions:

1. Cream sugar and butter till fluffy and light in a small bowl; beat in vanilla and egg whites.

2. Mix salt, flour and baking powder; alternately with milk, add to creamed mixture slowly, beating well after each. Fill the paper-lined muffin cups to 2/3 full.

3. Mix cinnamon and sugar; sprinkle 1/4 tsp. on each cupcake. Bake for 16-18 minutes at 375° till inserted toothpick in middle exits clean; cool it for 10 minutes.

4. Transfer from pans onto wire racks; fully cool. Frosting: Cream cinnamon, vanilla and butter in a small bowl; beat in confectioners' sugar slowly. Add milk; beat till fluffy and light.

5. Frost cupcakes; sprinkle extra cinnamon.

Nutrition:

Calories: 280 kcal

Carbohydrate: 44 g

Fat: 11 g

Protein: 3 g

Sodium: 201 mg

88. Little Pistachio Cakes

Preparation Time: 25 Minutes

Cooking Time: 15 Minutes

Servings: 12

Ingredients

- 175g butter, lightly salted
- 75g plain flour
- 140g pistachios plus a few for garnish
- 1 tbsp baking powder
- 175g golden caster sugar
- 2 tbsp vanilla extract
- 2 tbsp milk

For the icing

- 290g tub cream cheese
- 50g butter, lightly salted
- 100g icing sugar

Directions

1. Preheat oven to 350ºF. Grease muffin tins with oil then dust with flour and set aside. Place the pistachios in a food processor and pulse until fine but not greasy.
2. Add the rest of the cake ingredients and pulse until creamy. Scoop the mixture into the muffin tins up to two-thirds full. Bake for 15 minutes or until firm. let cool on a cooling rack.
3. Meanwhile, make the icing. Add 3 tbsp of cream cheese and butter in a small bowl then use a hand mixer to blend until smooth.
4. Add the remaining cream cheese and icing sugar then continue blending until smooth. Transfer into a piping bag. Pipe the icing on the cakes then sprinkle with chopped pistachios.
5. Serve and enjoy or preserve up to 3 days.

Nutrition

Calories 444 kcal; Fat 33g; Carbs 30g; Protein 5g; Fiber 1g

89.White Chococonut Cupcakes

Preparation Time: 15 Minutes

Cooking Time: 41 Minutes

Servings: 12

Ingredients:

- 1 tsp. butter, or as needed
- 2 cups baking mix
- 1 cup milk
- 1/3 cup white sugar
- 1 egg, beaten
- 2 tbsps. vegetable oil
- 1 cup sweetened flaked coconut
- 3/4 cup white chocolate chips, divided

Directions:

1. Set the oven to 400 0 F (200 0 C) and preheat. Coat a muffin tin with butter.
2. In a bowl, mix together vegetable oil, egg, sugar, milk and baking mix. Stlr well. Fold in 1/4 cup of chocolate chips and 3/4 cup of coconut flakes. Fill the buttered tin with batter; add the rest of coconut flakes to scatter on top. Put in the prepared oven and bake cupcakes for 15 to 18 minutes until when you insert a toothpick into the center, it should come out clean. Let it cool for about 10 minutes.
3. In a microwave-safe glass or ceramic bowl, melt the remaining half a cup chocolate chips in 15-second intervals, stirring after each melting, about 1 minute.
4. Drizzle over cooled cupcakes with melted chocolate.

Nutrition:

Calories: 234 kcal; Carbohydrate: 28.4 g; Cholesterol: 20 mg; Fat: 12.1 g

90.Strawberry Brownies

Preparation Time: 10 Minutes

Cooking Time: 40 Minutes

Servings: 10

Ingredients

- 1 egg
- 1 cup melted butter, cooled
- 1 tablespoon vanilla extract
- 1 pound sliced fresh strawberries, divided
- 1 cup sugar
- 1/2 cup cocoa powder
- 1 1/2 cups cake flour, more as needed

Directions:

1. Preheat oven to 350 degrees F (175 degrees C). Lightly grease a 9-inch pie plate. Whisk together egg, melted butter, and vanilla in a large bowl. Puree about 1/4 cup of the sliced strawberries and whisk into the butter. Sift together the sugar, cocoa powder, and cake flour.
2. Fold into the butter, and mix until well incorporated. Use more flour if needed to end up with a mixture in between a cake batter and a cookie dough (the strawberries will add additional moisture).
3. Gently fold in the remaining sliced strawberries and pour the batter into prepared pie plate.
4. Bake in preheated oven until a toothpick inserted into the center comes out clean, 30 to 40 minutes.

Nutrition:

Calorie: 320; Fat: 13; Carbs: 49; Sodium: 330 mg; Protein: 4 g

Conclusion

Baking is a great creative outlet and a great way to let off steam. If you're learning how to bake, you will find that working with the dough and pounding it out is a great way to let off the steam of a long school day or a long week. Stressed out thinking about report cards or that exam? Try beating up some pizza dough until you can make something amazingly delicious out of it.

Baking new and wonderful things from all around the world can show you a lot about the flavors and customs that come from all over the world. Learning about new cultures and their customs helps us to be more connected as a human race, and allows us to be more open to other new experiences in the future.

Buying brownies, for instance, at the bakery can cost as much as $15 for a nice, big batch! When you make your own brownies at home, whether from a mix or from scratch, you will be saving an average of about a dollar per brownie! With savings like that, it's a wonder anyone ever lets professionals do their baking for them, right?

Well, if you get nice and experienced at making dishes on your own, you can be the person that all your friends and family call when they're looking for the most delicious goods that anyone can make!

You can also bake for yourself and keep your favorite delicious treats on hand whenever you want them. Could you imagine having homemade chocolate chip cookies in the kitchen all the time because you made a batch, and they're still around for you to snack on? Jackpot!

Baking with the people that we know and love can be such a wonderful bonding experience. Learning together, rolling up your sleeves, talking about the recipe, getting to know more about how baking works and how each of the ingredients interact with one another and working together to make something truly delicious is a wonderful way to spend time with someone that you care about.

Consider finding a recipe that you and friends can follow the next time they come over to visit, once you've gained a little bit of cooking skill of your own. Consider having an adult help you to roll out your own dough to make biscuits or croissants for the morning after an awesome sleepover with your friends.

When you start to learn more about baking, and you start to remember how to make certain things on your own, you will find that you can express yourself and make your own wonderful creations in the kitchen. What an excellent feeling.

You will want to make sure that you try lots of new things in the kitchen to discover new flavors, new recipes, new foods, and to push the boundaries of what you know.

Baking is such a great passion to have and there are so many resources out there for you to use. Always look out for new skills that you can learn to make your time in the kitchen more fun and more rewarding.

DESSERT COOKBOOK FOR TEENS

A Simple Recipe Book for Delicious Cakes, Cookies, Ice Cream, Puddings and Tarts for Kids and Teenagers to Enjoy with the Whole Family

Vicky Cooper

INTRODUCTION

Desserts, by definition, are meant to be special. We serve them at holiday meals, birthday celebrations, weddings, and other momentous occasions and, because of that, we want each one to stand out and be indulgent. Happily, there are plenty of easy-to-make desserts that are just perfect for celebrating any number of occasions. This book is loaded with such recipes—from cookies, brownies, and bars to candies and other confections.

MAKING DESSERT TECHNIQUES AND SKILLS
- Read the recipe in its entirety before starting.
- Preheat the oven. Preheating the oven before baking is essential
- Use the appropriate measuring cups for liquid and dry ingredients.
- Let your ingredients come to room temperature before starting the recipe.
- Temper ingredients when mixing hot with cold.
- Do not overwork the dough once flour has been added.
- Grease the baking sheet or pan, or use parchment paper to line it.
- Bake on the oven's middle rack.
- Check for doneness at the minimum time.
- Let baked goods cool properly.

Equipment's
- Baking sheet
- Rimmed baking
- Measuring cups & spoons
- Mixing bowls
- Electric mixer
- Whisk
- Rolling pin
- Pastry
- Parchment paper
- Wire rack
- Cookie scoops.

- Silicone baking mats
- Stand mixer
- Scale

MEASURING LIQUIDS

Transparent measuring cups are best to use for larger amounts of liquids; measuring spoons work for smaller amounts. Pour liquids directly into the measuring cup and place on a flat surface such as your counter. Here's the trick: To check your measurement, be sure to bend down and look at the liquid at eye level. Looking from below or above can result in a miscalculation. When using measuring spoons, fill the spoon until it's level and flat all the way across.

MEASURING DRY INGREDIENTS

1. The most accurate method for measuring dry ingredients is by using a scale and measuring by weight, not volume, especially for flour. However, most recipes call for measuring by volume (including those in this book). Use dry measuring cups for larger amounts of dry ingredients, and measuring spoons for smaller amounts. Dry measuring cups are typically opaque (not transparent) and made of metal or plastic.
2. To measure flour, lightly spoon the flour directly into the measuring cup. Using the flat side of a butter knife, gently scrape the excess off so the flour is level with the measuring cup.
3. Brown sugar is usually measured by packing the brown sugar into the measuring cup tightly, unless otherwise noted. You can press it down so it's level, or with the flat side of a butter knife, gently scrape off the excess to make it level.
4. For most other dry ingredients, you can use the measuring cup to scoop up the ingredients and shake it a bit until level with the measuring cup.

MIXING

1. Mixing means to stir the ingredients together until they are combined, and it can be done by hand or with an electric mixer. Folding means to combine the ingredients softly to avoid overmixing.

Creaming Butter and Sugar
1. Creaming is the process of beating air into butter, which provides structure for baked goods. Sugar is responsible for "punching" holes in the butter and creating air pockets. Always use softened butter. Creaming can be done by hand or with a mixer.

Whipping Egg Whites
1. Whipping egg whites adds air into the whites to lighten them into a fluffy cloud. Whipped egg whites can be used for meringues or to help cakes rise.

Cutting Butter into Flour
1. Cutting in means to incorporate butter into flour. It is the key to making tender, flaky pastries, biscuits, and pie crusts. Unless otherwise stated in the recipe, always use cold butter, preferably cut into small cubes. If you don't have a pastry blender, you can also use a food processor for this task, but be sure to pulse the butter into the flour, so as not to overwork the dough

CONVERSION TABLE
Volume Equivalents (Liquid)

US STANDARD	US STANDARD (OUNCES)	METRIC (APPROXIMATE)
2 tablespoons	1 fl. oz.	30 mL
¼ cup	2 fl. oz.	60 mL
½ cup	4 fl. oz.	120 mL
1 cup	8 fl. oz.	240 mL
1½ cups	12 fl. oz.	355 mL
2 cups or 1 pint	16 fl. oz.	475 mL
4 cups or 1 quart	32 fl. oz.	1 L
1 gallon	128 fl. oz.	4 L

Oven Temperatures
FAHRENHEIT(F)   CELSIUS (C) (APPROXIMATE)

250°F	120°C
300°F	150°C
325°F	165°C
350°F	180°C
375°F	190°C
400°F	200°C
425°F	220°C
450°F	230°C

Volume Equivalents (Dry)

US STANDARD	METRIC (APPROXIMATE)
⅛ teaspoon	0.5 mL
¼ teaspoon	1 mL
½ teaspoon	2 mL
¾ teaspoon	4 mL
1 teaspoon	5 mL
1 tablespoon	15 mL
¼ cup	59 mL
⅓ cup	79 mL
½ cup	118 mL
⅔ cup	156 mL
¾ cup	177 mL
1 cup	235 mL
2 cups or 1 pint	475 mL
3 cups	700 mL
4 cups or 1 quart	1 L

Weight Equivalents

US STANDARD	METRIC (APPROXIMATE)
½ ounce	15 g
1 ounce	30 g
2 ounces	60 g
4 ounces	115 g
8 ounces	225 g
12 ounces	340 g
16 ounces or 1 pound	455 g

CHAPTER 1: SWEET RECIPE FOR BREAKFAST

91. Dark Chocolate Energy Bites

Preparation Time: 20 Minutes
Cooking Time: 0 Minutes
Servings: 20 – 25

INGREDIENTS

- one cup dried oatmeal
- 2/3 cup toasted coconut flakes
- half cup cashew butter
- half cup ground flaxseed
- half cup dark chocolate chips (or cacao nibs)
- one-third cup honey either agave nectar
- 1 tsp. vanilla extract

DIRECTIONS

1. Stir all ingredients along in a medium bowl till thoroughly mixed. Overlay and allow chill within the refrigerator for half some hour. As chilled, roll into balls of whatever size you would like. (Mine were approximately 1" in diameter.) Keep in some airtight container and keep refrigerated for up to one week. Makes approximately 20-25 balls.

NUTRITION: Calorie: 89.6 kcal Fat: 5.1 g Carbs: 11.9 g Sodium: 21.3 mg Protein: 2.4 g

92. Peanut Butter Chocolate

Preparation Time: 10 Minutes
Cooking Time: 15 Minutes
Servings: 12

INGREDIENTS

- 1.5 cups white whole lukewarmth flour
- 2 tsps. baking powder
- 1 tsp salt
- 1 egg
- 1 2/3 cups Almond Breeze original almond milk
- One-quarter cup creamy peanut butter
- 1 tbsp honey either agave
- 1 tsp vanilla extract
- One-quarter cup mini semisweet chocolate chips
- (if you want toppings: extra liquified peanut butter, extra chocolate chips, and/or maple syrup)

DIRECTIONS

1. In a big mixing bowl, blend along flour, baking powder and salt till mix. put aside. In a different mixing bowl, blend along egg, Almond Breeze, peanut butter, honey, and vanilla extract till mixed. Rain the peanut butter mix into the flour mix, and blend till simply mixed. (Watch oneself not to over-mix the batter.) Lukewarmth a big sauté pan over medium-low heat. Just as hot, slightly spatter the pan with cooking spray. Peel One-quarter cup of pancake batter into the pan for each pancake, then strew one tsp of chocolate chips on top. prepare till the pancakes start to bubble and the edges begin to set, one half mins. Flip the pancakes over and prepare the second side till golden, one half mins. Place prepared pancakes to a different plate. recur with the remaining batter.
2. Serve hot. Drizzled with extra peanut butter and chocolate chips (and/or maple syrup) supposing desired.

NUTRITION: : Calorie:44 kcal Fat: 2.8 g Carbs: 4 g Sodium: 17 mg Protein: 0.8 g

93. Simple Crepes

Preparation Time: 10 Minutes
Cooking Time: 20 Minutes
Servings: 4

INGREDIENTS

- 1 C. all-purpose flour
- 2 eggs
- 1/2 C. milk
- 1/2 C. water
- 1/4 tsp salt
- 2 tbsps. butter, melted

DIRECTIONS

1. In a large bowl, add the eggs and flour and beat till well combined. Slowly, add the water and milk, beating continuously till well combined. Add the butter and salt and beat till smooth. Lightly, grease a frying pan and heat it on medium-high heat. Place about 1/4 C. of the mixture and tilt the pan to spread it evenly. Cook for about 2 minutes. Carefully, flip the crepe and cook till golden brown. Repeat with the remaining mixture. Serve hot.

NUTRITION: Calories 216 kcal Fat 9.2 g Carbohydrates 25.5 g Protein 7.4 g Sodium 235 mg

94. Raspberry-Yogurt Waffle Bowl

Preparation Time: 10 Minutes

Cooking Time: 14 Minutes

Servings: 2

INGREDIENTS:

- 1 egg, beaten
- 1 tbsp almond flour
- ¼ cup finely grated mozzarella cheese
- ¼ tsp baking powder
- 1 cup Greek yogurt
- 1 cup fresh raspberries
- 2 tbsp almonds, chopped

DIRECTIONS:

1. Preheat a waffle bowl maker and grease lightly with cooking spray. Meanwhile, in a medium bowl, whisk all the ingredients except the yogurt, raspberries until smooth batter forms.
2. Open the iron, pour in half of the mixture, cover, and cook until crispy, 6 to 7 minutes.
3. Remove the waffle bowl onto a plate and set aside. Make the second waffle bowl with the remaining batter. To serve, divide the yogurt into the waffle bowls and top with the raspberries and almonds.

NUTRITION: : Calories 75 kcal Fats 3.69 g Carbs 6.95 g Protein 4.07 g

95. Yogurt, Honey & Banana Filled Crepes

Preparation Time: 15 Minutes

Cooking Time: 15 Minutes

Servings: 4

INGREDIENTS

- 1 3/4 C. fat-free milk
- 3/4 C. flour
- 1 egg
- 1 egg white
- 2 tbsps. honey, divided
- 1 (8 ounce) container low-fat banana yogurt
- 1 banana, diced
- 1/2 tsp vanilla extract
- Fresh mint sprigs
- Powdered sugar

DIRECTIONS

1. In a bowl, add the egg, egg whites, flour and 1 tbsp of honey and beat till well combined and keep aside for About 10 minutes. Lightly, grease a skillet and heat on medium heat. Place about 1/4 C. of the mixture and tilt the pan to spread it evenly. Cook everything on both sides till golden brown. Repeat with the remaining mixture. In a blender, add the remaining honey, yogurt and vanilla and pulse till smooth. Transfer the yogurt mixture into a bowl and fold in chopped banana. Divide the banana mixture in the center of the crepes evenly and roll around the filling. Serve with a topping of powdered sugar and mint if you like.

NUTRITION: Calories 260 kcal Fat 1.6 g Carbohydrates 50.6g Protein 11.6 g Sodium   114 mg

96. Apple Filled Crepes

Preparation Time: 30 Minutes
Cooking Time: 30 Minutes
Servings: 8

INGREDIENTS

- 3 eggs
- 1/4 tsp salt
- 2 C. all-purpose flour
- 2 C. milk
- 1/4 C. vegetable oil
- 1/2 tsp ground cinnamon
- 4 Granny Smith apples, peeled and diced
- 1/2 C. white sugar
- 2 tsps. cinnamon
- 2 tbsps. water
- 2 tbsps. cornstarch
- 1 tbsp water
- 1 1/2 tbsps. milk
- 8 tsps. vegetable oil, divided

DIRECTIONS

1. In a bowl, add the eggs and salt and beat well. Slowly, add the flour, beating continuously, followed by 2 C. of milk till well combined. Add 1/4 C. of the oil and 1/2 tsp of the cinnamon and beat till smooth and refrigerate, covered for at least 1 hour. In another bowl, mix together the apples, 2 tbsps. of the water, sugar and the remaining cinnamon. In a small bowl, mix together the cornstarch and remaining water and transfer the mixture into the bowl of the apple mixture. In a pan, add the apples mixture on medium heat and cook, stirring occasionally for about 8-10 minutes. Grease a crepe pan with 1 tsp of oil and heat on medium heat. Place about 1/3 C. of the mixture and tilt the pan to spread it evenly. Cook for about 30 seconds and carefully, flip it. Cook till golden brown. Repeat with the remaining mixture. Divide the apple mixture in the center of the crepes evenly and roll around the filling. Serve immediately.

NUTRITION: Calories 361 k Cal Fat 14.8 g Carbohydrates 50.4gProtein 7.9 g Sodium 127 mg

97. Maple Fruity Compote

Preparation Time: 5 Minutes

Cooking Time: 25 Minutes

Servings: 6

INGREDIENTS

- 3 tbsps. butter
- 2 tbsps. maple sugar
- 2 tsps. grated fresh ginger
- 1 tsp ground cinnamon
- 1/2 tsp freshly grated nutmeg
- 3 C. frozen peach slices
- 1 C. frozen blackberries

DIRECTIONS

1. In a pan, melt the butter on medium heat. Add the ginger, maple syrup and spices and stir to combine. Stir in the peach slices and cook, stirring occasionally for about 20 minutes. Gently, stir in the blackberries and cook for about 5 minutes.

NUTRITION: Calories 100 kcal Fat 6 g Carbs 12.1gProtein 0.4 g Sodium 44 mg

98. Apple Pie Waffles

Preparation Time: 10 Minutes
Cooking Time: 30 Minutes
Servings: 4

INGREDIENTS

- 1 3/4 cups whole wheat flour
- 1/2 cup wheat bran
- 1/2 tsp. salt
- 1 tsp. apple pie spice
- 3/4 cup water
- 1 tsp. honey
- 2 tsps. active dry yeast
- 2 medium apples, grated
- 3 tbsps. applesauce
- 1 cup skim milk
- 2 egg whites

DIRECTION

1. Combine the salt, flour, apple pie spice, and wheat bran together in a medium-sized bowl. Put it aside. Mix the honey and water together in another bowl. Put the yeast on the top surface of the honey mixture and allow it to rest for about 5 minutes until dissolved. Once the yeast has been fully dissolved, put in the milk, apples, egg whites, and applesauce and mix until everything is thoroughly combined. Add the prepared apple mixture into the flour mixture and mix well. Cover the mixture and allow it to sit for about 15 minutes. Let the waffle iron heat up and use a cooking spray to grease it. Pour the prepared batter mixture onto the waffle iron following the manufacturer's suggested amount. Shut the waffle iron close and let it bake for about 7 minutes or until there's no more steam coming out from the waffle iron and you can already remove the baked waffle with ease. Do the same for the rest of the batter mixture.

NUTRITION INFORMATION: Calories: 276 k Cal Carbs: 59.4 g Fat: 1.6 g Protein: 13.2 g Sodium: 349 mg

99. Birthday Cake Waffles

Preparation Time: 20 Minutes
Cooking Time: 40 Minutes
Servings: 6

INGREDIENTS

- 1 cup all-purpose flour
- 1 cup (about 5 oz.) confetti cake mix or flavor of choice
- 2 tbsps. cornstarch
- 3 tsps. baking powder
- 1/4 tsp. salt
- 2 tbsps. rainbow sprinkles, optional
- 2 large eggs
- 1-3/4 cups 2% milk
- 3/4 to 1 cup plain Greek yogurt
- 1/2 tsp. vanilla extract
- 1/2 tsp. almond extract

Cream Cheese Frosting:

- 4 oz. softened cream cheese or reduced-fat cream cheese
- 1/4 cup butter, softened
- 1-1/2 to 2 cups confectioners' sugar
- 1/2 tsp. vanilla extract
- 1 to 3 tbsps. 2% milk

DIRECTION

1. Set the oven to 300°. Mix together the first 5 ingredients with rainbow sprinkles, if wanted. Whisk together extracts, yogurt, milk and eggs in another bowl, then put into the flour mixture and blend until smooth. Preheat waffle maker coated with cooking spray then follow the manufacturer's instructions to bake waffles until turn golden brown. Turn cooked waffles to oven until serving. To make frosting, beat together butter and cream cheese for 2 to 3 minutes on high, until fluffy and light. Beat in confectioners' sugar gradually with 1/2 cup at a time, until smooth, then beat in vanilla. Put in enough milk to get the wanted consistency. Spread over warm waffles. Quarter the waffles and stack them, then garnish with birthday candles, if you want a cakelike look.

NUTRITION: Calories: 528 calories Carbs: 72 g Fat: 22 g Protein: 10 g Sodium: 695 mg

100.　Banana Hazelnut Waffles

Preparation Time: 20 Minutes

Cooking Time: 25 Minutes

Servings: 12

INGREDIENTS

- 1 cup all-purpose flour
- 1/2 cup whole wheat flour
- 2 tbsps. flaxseed
- 1-1/2 tsps. baking powder
- 1/2 tsp. salt
- 3 eggs, separated
- 1 cup milk
- 1/2 cup mashed ripe banana
- 2 tbsps. orange juice
- 1 tbsp. butter, melted
- 1 tsp. vanilla extract
- 1/2 cup chopped hazelnuts
- 1-1/2 cups maple pancake syrup
- 1 tbsp. hazelnut Belgian cafe coffee drink mix
- Sliced ripe bananas and hazelnuts, optional

DIRECTION

1. Mix together salt, baking powder, flax and flours in a big bowl. Whisk together vanilla, butter, orange juice, banana, milk and egg yolks in another big bowl. Stir the wet mixture into flour mixture until moist, then stir in hazelnuts. Beat egg whites in a big bowl until create stiff peaks, then fold into the batter. Following the manufacturer's ingredients, bake in a preheated waffle iron until turning golden brown. At the same time, mix coffee drink mix with syrup in a small saucepan, then heat through. Serve together with waffles and decorate with hazelnuts as well as bananas, if wanted.

NUTRITION: Calories: 493 kcal Carbs: 86 g Fat: 14 g Protein: 10 g Sodium: 431 mg

101. Blueberry Oat Waffles

Preparation Time: 15 Minutes

Cooking Time: 25

Servings: 2

INGREDIENTS

- 2/3 cup all-purpose flour
- 1/2 cup quick-cooking oats
- 1 tbsp. brown sugar
- 1 tsp. baking powder
- 1/2 tsp. salt
- 2/3 cup milk
- 1 egg
- 1/4 cup canola oil
- 1/2 tsp. lemon juice
- 1/4 cup ground pecans
- 1/2 cup fresh or frozen blueberries

DIRECTION

1. Mix together salt, baking powder, brown sugar, oats and flour in a bowl. Mix together lemon juice, oil, egg and milk, then stir into dry ingredients and blend well. Fold in blueberries and pecans, then allow to stand about 5 minutes. Following the manufacturer's directions to bake in the preheated waffle iron until turn golden brown.

NUTRITION: Calories: 669 kcal Carbs: 62 g Fat: 41 g Protein: 15 g Sodium: 866 mg

CHAPTER 2: CAKES AND CUPCAKES RECIPE

102. Lemon Pudding Cake

Preparation Time: 15 Minutes
Cooking Time: 60 Minutes
Servings: 8

INGREDIENTS

- Butter, for greasing
- 4 eggs, at room temperature, separated
- ¾ cup sugar
- ½ cup unsalted butter, melted
- 1 teaspoon vanilla extract
- ¾ cup all-purpose flour
- Zest of 1 lemon
- ¼ cup freshly squeezed lemon juice
- 1¾ cups (whole or low-fat) milk, warm but not hot
- Confectioners' sugar, for garnish

DIRECTIONS

1. Preheat the oven to 325°F. Coat the cakepan with butter. In the bowl of a stand mixer or in a large mixing bowl using an electric mixer, whip the egg whites until they form stiff peaks. In a separate large mixing bowl, whisk together the egg yolks and sugar until the mixture becomes pale. Add the melted butter and

vanilla, and beat to combine. Add the flour, and mix until it is fully incorporated. Add the lemon zest and juice, and beat to mix. With the mixer running, add the milk. Using a rubber spatula, gently fold in the whipped egg whites, about one-third at a time, until they are mostly incorporated. Transfer the batter to the prepared cake pan, and bake in the preheated oven for 45 to 60 minutes, until the top is firm to the touch. Remove the cake pan from the oven, and let the cake cool completely on a wire rack. Sprinkle confectioners' sugar over the top, and serve at room temperature.

NUTRITION: Calorie: 290 kcal Fat: 3 g Carbs: 30 g Sodium: 230 mg Protein: 3 g

103. Pineapple Dump Cake

With Coconut Frosting

Preparation Time: 10 Minutes
Cooking Time: 40 Minutes
Servings: 12

INGREDIENTS

For the Cake

- Nonstick cooking spray
- 2 cups all-purpose flour
- 2 teaspoons baking soda
- 2 cups granulated sugar
- 2 eggs
- ½ teaspoon vanilla extract
- 2½ cups canned crushed pineapple, with juice

For the Frosting

- ½ cup (1 stick) unsalted butter
- ¾ cup evaporated milk
- 1 cup granulated sugar
- 1½ cups sweetened shredded coconut

DIRECTIONS:

1. Preheat the oven to 350°F. Spray the baking pan with cooking spray. In a large mixing bowl, stir together the flour, baking soda, sugar, eggs, vanilla, and crushed pineapple with its juice. Transfer the batter to the prepared baking pan, and bake in the preheated oven for 30 to 40 minutes, until the center of the cake is set. While the cake is baking, in a saucepan over medium heat, combine the butter, evaporated milk, and sugar and cook, stirring frequently, until the mixture thickens, about 5 minutes. Stir in the coconut. Remove the cake from the oven and immediately poke a dozen or so holes in it using a skewer or chopstick. Pour the hot frosting over the cake, and serve warm or at room temperature.

NUTRITION: Calorie: 125 kcal Fat: 4.2 g Carbs: 19.1 g Sodium: 54.2 g Protein: 86. 3 mg

104. Crumbled Cupcakes

Preparation Time: 25 minutes
Cooking Time: 3 hours
Servings:4

INGREDIENTS

- 1 cup almond flour
- 1 teaspoon vanilla extract
- 1 teaspoon ground cinnamon
- 4 tablespoons butter, frozen
- 1 teaspoon ricotta cheese
- 1 tablespoon Erythritol
- 1 tablespoon strawberries, chopped

DIRECTIONS

1. Mix up together Erythritol and strawberries. Mash the mixture. Then grate the frozen butter and mix it up with almond flour, vanilla extract, and ground cinnamon. Add ricotta cheese and knead the dough. After this, transfer the dough in the freezer for 20 minutes. Remove the dough from the freezer and grated it. Place 1 tablespoon of grated dough in the muffin mold. Then add mashed strawberries. Add 1 tablespoon of dough again. Repeat the same steps for all muffin molds. After this, arrange the cupcakes in the crockpot. Close the lid and cook them on High for 3 hours.

NUTRITION: Calories 149 kcal Fat 15.1 g Carbs 6.1 g Protein 1.8 g

105. Pumpkin Cake

Preparation Time: 30 Minutes
Cooking Time: 1 Hour
Servings: 8

INGREDIENTS:

- 1 cup packed shredded pumpkin, plus more for topping
- ½ cup chopped walnuts
- 2 cups water
- 1 cup flour
- ⅔ cup sugar
- ½ cup half-and-half
- ¼ cup olive oil
- 3 eggs
- 1 teaspoon baking powder
- 1 teaspoon vanilla extract
- 1 teaspoon ground cinnamon
- ½ teaspoon ground nutmeg

Frosting:

- 4 ounces cream cheese, room temperature
- ½ cup confectioner sugar
- 8 tablespoon butter
- ½ teaspoon vanilla extract
- ⅛ teaspoon salt

DIRECTIONS:

1. In a bowl, beat eggs and sugar to get a smooth mixture; mix in oil, flour, vanilla extract, cinnamon, half-and-half, baking powder, and nutmeg. Stir well to obtain a fluffy batter; fold walnuts and pumpkin through the batter. Add batter into a 6-inch cake pan and cover with aluminum foil.
2. Into the pot, add water and set the reversible rack over the water. Lay cakepan gently onto the trivet. Close the crisping lid and select Bake/Roast; adjust the temperature to 250°F and the cook time to 40 minutes. Press Start. Beat cream cheese, confectioners' sugar, salt, vanilla extract, and butter in a mixing bowl until smooth; place in the refrigerator until needed for use.
3. Remove cake from the pan and transfer to the cooking wire rack to cool. Over the cake, spread frosting and apply a topping of shredded carrots, as desired.

NUTRITION: Calorie: 188 kcal Fat: 32. G Carbs: 33.8 g Sodium: 333.3 mg Protein: 7.1 g

106. Red Velvet Cupcakes

Preparation Time: 25 Minutes
Cooking Time: 15 Minutes
Servings: 12

INGREDIENTS

- 150g plain flour
- 1 tbsp cocoa powder
- 1 tbsp bicarbonate of soda
- 50g butter, soft
- 150g caster sugar
- 1 egg, beaten
- 1 tbsp vanilla paste
- 100ml buttermilk or kefir
- 50ml vegetable oil
- 1 tbsp white wine vinegar
- 1 tbsp red gel food coloring

For Cream Cheese Icing

- 100gbutter, slightly salted and softened
- 225g icing sugar
- 100 full fat cream cheese, stir to loosen

DIRECTIONS

1. Line your cupcake tins with 12 cupcakes cases then set aside. Preheat oven to 350⁰F. Sieve flour, cocoa powder, bicarbonate, and a pinch of salt in a mixing bowl. In a separate bowl, beat butter, sugar, egg, vanilla paste, milk, oil, and vinegar until well combined. Add the wet ingredients into the dry ingredients and mix until combined. Mix in the food coloring until you achieve your desired color. Divide the batter among the cupcake cases then bake for 15 minutes. Insert a skewer into the center. It should come out clean. Meanwhile, prepare the icing. Beat butter and icing sugar until fluffy then beat in cream cheese until well combined. Once the cake has fully cooled, use a piping bag to cover the cake top with the icing. Serve and enjoy.

NUTRITION: Calories 339 kcal Fat 17 g Carbs 42 g Protein 3 g Fiber 1 g

107. Vegan Cupcakes

Preparation Time: 30 Minutes
Cooking Time: 20 Minutes
Servings: 12

INGREDIENTS

- 150ml soy milk
- 1/2 tbsp cider vinegar
- 110 sunflower spread
- 110g caster sugar
- 1 tbsp vanilla extract
- 110g self-rising flour
- 1/2 tbsp baking powder

For the buttercream

- 125g vegan butter
- 250g icing sugar
- 1-1/4 tbsp vanilla extract
- Drops of vegan food coloring

DIRECTIONS

1. Preheat the oven to 350⁰F. Line the cupcake holes with paper cases then set aside. Add milk and vinegar in jag then stir. Let rest for some few minutes to thicken. In a mixing bowl, beat sunflower spread, sugar until well combined. Whisk in vanilla extract, flour, baking powder, and a pinch of salt until you get a creamy mixture. Divide the mixture among the cupcake cases, two-third full then bake for 20 minutes. Let the cupcakes cool on a wire rack. Meanwhile, beat vegan butter, icing sugar, and vanilla until pale and creamy. Add the desired food coloring then pipe on the cool cupcakes. Serve and enjoy.

NUTRITION: Calories 265 kcal Fat 12 g Carbs 37 g Protein 1 g Fiber 0.4 g

108. Easy Chocolate Cupcakes

Preparation Time: 10 Minutes
Cooking Time: 20 Minutes
Servings: 10

INGREDIENTS

- 300g dark chocolate, break into chunks
- 200g self-rising flour
- 200g light muscovado sugar
- 6 tbsp cocoa
- 150ml sunflower oil
- 284ml pot soured cream
- 2 eggs
- 1 tbsp vanilla extract
- 3 tbsp light muscovado sugar for icing

DIRECTIONS

1. Preheat the oven to 350°F. Line the cupcake tins with papers case then set-aside. Whizz 100g of chocolate chips into small pieces in your food processor. Add flour, sugar, cocoa, sunflower oil, 100ml cream, eggs, vanilla and 100ml water in a mixing bowl. Use a hand mixer to mix until smooth and well combined. Stir in the whizzed chocolate chips then divides the mixture among the cases. Bake for 20 minutes then place on a cooling rack. To make the icing, mix the remaining chocolate chips, cream, 3 tbsp sugar in a saucepan. Gently heat until the chocolate chips melts. Chill the icing in a fridge then swirl it on the cupcake. Serve and enjoy.

NUTRITION: Calories 534 kcal Fat 31 g Carbs 62 g Protein 6 g

109.   Coconut and Raspberry cupcakes

Preparation Time: 25 Minutes
Cooking Time: 20 Minutes
Servings: 12

INGREDIENTS

- 175g self-rising flour
- 140g caster sugar
- 50g desiccated coconut
- 140g butter softened
- 1/2 tbsp vanilla extract
- 2 eggs
- 4 tbsp milk
- 140g raspberry

For the Frosting

- 280g icing sugar
- 85g butter, soft
- 4 tbsp raspberry coulis
- Shredded or desiccated coconut for garnish

DIRECTIONS:

1. Preheat oven to 375ºF. Line the cupcakes tins with paper cases then set aside. Add the cake ingredients except for the raspberries in a mixing bowl then beat until light and fluffy. Fold in the raspberries then divide the mixture among the cake cases. Bake for 20 minutes or until firm to touch. Place the cakes on a cooling rack to cool. Beat sugar, butter, and raspberry coulis until light and fluffy in a bowl. Pipe onto the cakes then sprinkle the shredded coconut. Serve and enjoy.

NUTRITION: Calories 314 kcal Fat 17 g Carbs 37 g Protein 3 g Fiber 2 g

110. Carrot Cakes with Orange and Honey Syrup

Preparation Time: 15 Minutes
Cooking Time: 20 Minutes
Servings: 12

INGREDIENTS

- 175g light muscovado sugar
- 200g self-rising flour
- 1 tbsp bicarbonate of soda
- 2 tbsp mixed spice
- 1 orange, zested and juiced
- 2 eggs
- 150ml sunflower oil
- 50g natural yogurt
- 200g carrots, peeled and grated

For the syrup and icing

- 50 ml runny honey
- 150g mascarpone
- 100g thick natural yogurt
- 75g icing sugar sieved
- Edible flowers or orange zest for garnish

DIRECTIONS

1. Preheat the oven to 350⁰F. Grease muffin tins with oil then set aside. Mix sugar, flour bicarbonate, spice mix, and orange zest in a mixing bowl. In a separate bowl, whisk together eggs, sunflower oil, and yogurt until well combined. Stir in the wet ingredients into the dry ingredients along with the carrots.

Divide the mixture among the tins then bake for 22 minutes. Turn the cake out on a cooling rack and leave them to cool. Meanwhile, heat honey and orange juice in a saucepan. Let it boil then simmer until it turns syrupy. Spoon the syrup on each cake and let it cool. Make the icing by mixing mascarpone, natural yogurt, and icing sugar until well mixed. Swirl the icing on the cakes then garnish with flowers. Serve and enjoy.

NUTRITION: Calories 356 kcal Fat 20 g Carbs 39 g Protein 4g Fiber 1g

CHAPTER 3: COOKIES, BROWNIES AND BARS

111.   Chewy Fudge Drop Cookies

Preparation Time: 20 Minutes
Cooking Time: 30 Minutes
Servings: 4 dozen

INGREDIENTS:

- 1 cup (6 oz.) semisweet chocolate chips, divided
- 3 tbsps. canola oil
- 1 cup packed brown sugar
- 3 egg whites
- 2 tbsps. plus 1-1/2 tsps. light corn syrup
- 1 tbsp. water
- 2-1/2 tsps. vanilla extract
- 1-3/4 cups all-purpose flour
- 2/3 cup plus 1 tbsp. confectioners' sugar, divided
- 1/3 cup baking cocoa
- 2-1/4 tsps. baking powder
- 1/8 tsp. salt

DIRECTIONS:

1. In the microwave, melt oil and three-fourths chocolate chips; whisk till smooth. Add to big bowl; let cool down for 5 minutes. Whisk in brown sugar. Put in vanilla, water, corn syrup and egg whites till becoming smooth. Mix salt, baking powder, cocoa, two-thirds cup of the confectioners' square, and flour; slowly put into the chocolate mixture till mixed. Whisk in rest of the chocolate chips. The dough would be very stiff. Drop by tablespoonfuls, 2 inches apart, to greased baking sheets. Bake at 350 degrees till becoming set and puffed or for 8 to 10 minutes. Let cool down for 2 minutes prior to transferring onto the wire racks. Sprinkle the cooled cookies with the rest of the confectioners' sugar.

NUTRITION: Calories: 139 calories Total Carbohydrate: 26 g Cholesterol: 0 mg Total Fat: 4 g Fiber: 1 g Protein: 2 g Sodium: 48 mg

112. Chocolate Fudge Peanut Butter Cookies

Preparation Time: 20 Minutes

Cooking Time: 30 Minutes

Servings: 3-1/2 dozen.

INGREDIENTS:

- 2 cans (16 oz. each) chocolate fudge frosting, divided
- 1 large egg
- 1 cup chunky peanut butter
- 1-1/2 cups all-purpose flour
- Granulated sugar

DIRECTIONS:

1. Preheat an oven to 375°; keep 1 can and 1/3 cup frosting to top cookies. Mix leftover frosting, peanut butter and egg till blended in big bowl; mix flour in till just moist. By rounded tablespoonfuls, drop dough on greased baking sheets, 2-in. apart; use fork dipped in sugar to flatten. Bake till set for 8-11 minutes. Transfer from pans to wire racks to fully cool; spread reserved frosting.

NUTRITION: Calories: 143 calories Total Carbohydrate: 18 g Cholesterol: 5 mg Total Fat: 7 g Fiber: 1 g Protein: 2 g Sodium: 79 mg Fudge

113. Bonbon Cookies

Preparation Time: 25 Minutes

Cooking Time: 35 Minutes

Servings: 5-1/2 dozen.

INGREDIENTS:

- 2 cups all-purpose flour
- 1/2 cup finely chopped pecans
- 2 cups (12 oz.) semisweet chocolate chips
- 1/4 cup butter, cubed
- 1 can (14 oz.) sweetened condensed milk
- 1 tsp. vanilla extract
- 1 package (12 oz.) milk chocolate kisses
- 2 oz. white baking chocolate
- 1 tsp. canola oil

DIRECTIONS:

1. Mix together flour and pecans in a large bowl; put aside. Melt chocolate chips and butter in a microwave-safe bowl; stir till smooth. Stir milk and vanilla into the mix until incorporated. Add into flour mixture and combine thoroughly. Set oven to preheat at 350°. Once the dough is cool enough to work with, shape a tablespoonful of this mixture around each chocolate kiss. Put them 1 inch apart onto ungreased baking sheets. Bake until tops begin to crack, for about 7-9 minutes. Let them cool down on wire racks. Melt white chocolate with oil in a microwave; stir till smooth. Drizzle on top of the cookies.

NUTRITION: Calories: 203 calories Total Carbohydrate: 26 g Cholesterol: 10 mg Total Fat: 11 g Fiber: 1 g Protein: 3 g Sodium: 41 mg

114. Caramel Fudge Brownies

Preparation Time: 15 Minutes

Cooking Time: 45 Minutes

Servings: 9

INGREDIENTS:

- 4 oz. unsweetened chocolate, chopped
- 3 egg whites, lightly beaten
- 1 cup sugar
- 2 jars (2-1/2 oz. each) prune baby food
- 1 tsp. vanilla extract
- 1/2 cup all-purpose flour
- 1/2 tsp. salt
- 1/4 cup chopped walnuts
- 6 tbsps. fat-free caramel ice cream topping
- 9 tbsps. reduced fat-whipped topping

DIRECTIONS:

1. Heat chocolate in a microwave until melted, then stir till smooth. Let it cool slightly. Whisk egg whites and sugar together in a large bowl. Mix in chocolate mixture, vanilla and prunes. Mix salt and flour; slowly add to the chocolate mixture just until the mixture become moist.
2. Spread the mixture onto a greased 8" square baking pan. Top with walnuts. Bake for 30-32 minutes at 350 degrees until the top is slightly springy to the touch.
3. Let sit on a wire rack to cool. Cut into squares and drizzle with caramel topping; drop a dollop of whipped topping on top.

NUTRITION: Calories: 251 calories Total Carbohydrate: 42 g Cholesterol: 0 mg Total Fat: 10 g Fiber: 3 g Protein: 4 g Sodium: 170 mg

115. Chocolate Chip Fudgy Brownies

Preparation Time: 15 Minutes

Cooking Time: 40 Minutes

Servings: 16-20

INGREDIENTS:

- 4 oz. unsweetened chocolate, chopped
- 1 cup butter, cubed
- 4 eggs
- 2 cups sugar
- 1 tsp. vanilla extract
- 1 cup all-purpose flour
- 1 cup (6 oz.) semisweet chocolate chips
- 1 cup chopped pecans, optional
- Confectioners' sugar

DIRECTIONS:

1. Melt butter and unsweetened chocolate in a microwave; mix until smooth. Whip the vanilla, sugar and eggs for 1-2 minutes in a big bowl or until light and lemon in color. Whip in chocolate mixture. Put flour; whip until just blended. Fold in pecans and chocolate chips (optional).
2. Put into a greased 13x9-inch baking dish. Bake for 25 to 30 mins at 350° or until a toothpick inserted in the middle comes out with moist crumbs. Let cool on a wire rack.
3. Slice into bars. Dust with confectioners' sugar to serve, or freeze. It can be in the freezer for up to 6 months.

NUTRITION: Calories: 239 calories Total Carbohydrate: 33 g Cholesterol: 5 mg Total Fat: 12 g Fiber: 1 g Protein: 2 g Sodium: 199 mg

116. Homemade Brownies

Preparation Time: 10 Minutes
Cooking Time: 55 Minutes
Servings: 9

INGREDIENTS:

- ¼ cup of water
- 1 ¼ cups of white sugar
- 2 ounces of unsweetened chocolate, chopped
- ¾ cup of all-purpose flour
- 1/3 cup of unsweetened powdered cocoa
- ½ cup of semi-sweet chocolate chips
- ¼ teaspoons of baking powder
- Dash of salt
- 2 eggs, beaten
- ½ cup of vegetable oil
- 1 teaspoon of pure vanilla

DIRECTIONS

1. Preheat the oven to 350 degrees. Place a sheet of parchment paper into a baking dish. Grease with cooking spray. Set the baking dish aside. In a saucepan set over low to medium heat, add in the white sugar, water and chopped unsweetened chocolate. Cook for 3 to 5 minutes or until melted. Stir well until smooth in consistency. Remove and set aside to cool. In a separate bowl, add in the all-purpose flour, powdered unsweetened cocoa, semi-sweet chocolate, baking powder and dash of salt. Stir well to mix. Add in the vegetable oil, beaten eggs and pure vanilla. Stir well to mix. Add in the chocolate mix into the flour mix. Stir well until just mixed. Pour into the baking dish. Place into the oven to bake for 40 minutes or until baked through. Remove and set aside to cool completely before serving.

NUTRITION: Calorie:112 kcal Fat: 1.8 g Carbs: 12 g Sodium: 82 mg Protein: 14 mg

117. Double Chocolate Brownies

Preparation Time: 10 Minutes
Cooking Time: 40 Minutes
Servings: 8

INGREDIENTS:

- 1 cup of butter
- 2 ¼ cups of white sugar
- 1 ¼ cups of powdered cocoa
- 1 teaspoon of salt
- 1 teaspoon of baking powder
- 1 tablespoon of pure vanilla
- 4 eggs
- 1 ½ cups of all-purpose flour
- 2 cups of semi-sweet chocolate chips

DIRECTIONS:

1. Preheat the oven to 350 degrees. Grease a baking dish with shortening. Set aside.
2. In a saucepan set over low heat, add in the butter. Once melted, add in the white sugar. Cook for 1 to 2 minutes. Remove from heat and transfer into a bowl.
3. Add in the powdered cocoa, dash of salt, pure vanilla, baking powder and eggs. Stir well until evenly mixed.
4. Add in the all-purpose flour and semi-sweet chocolate chips. Fold gently to incorporate.
5. Pour into the baking dish.
6. Place into the oven to bake for 30 minutes. Remove and set aside to cool completely.
7. Slice and serve.

NUTRITION: Calorie: 90 kcal Fat: 2.5 g Carbs: 18 g Sodium: 45 g Protein: 2 g

118. Mocha Brownies

Preparation Time: 10 Minutes
Cooking Time: 40 Minutes
Servings: 16

INGREDIENTS

- 1 cup of white sugar
- ½ cup of light brown sugar
- ¾ cup of butter, melted
- ¼ cup of brewed coffee
- ½ cup of powdered unsweetened cocoa
- 1 teaspoon of powdered espresso
- 3 eggs
- 1 teaspoon of pure vanilla
- 1 cup of all-purpose flour
- ¼ cup of walnuts, chopped

Ingredients for the glaze:

- 1 ½ Tablespoons of brewed coffee
- 1 cup of powdered sugar

Ingredients for garnish:

- ¼ cup of rainbow sprinkles

DIRECTIONS

1. Prepare the brownies. In a bowl, add in the melted butter. Add in the white sugar and light brown sugar. Cook in the microwave for 30 seconds. Stir well to mix. Transfer into the freezer to chill for 10 minutes.

2. Add in the brewed coffee, powdered cocoa, powdered espresso, eggs and pure vanilla. Whisk until smooth in consistency.

3. Add in the all-purpose flour and chopped walnuts. Stir well until just mixed.

4. Pour into an aluminum foil lined baking dish.

5. Place into the oven to bake for 25 to 30 minutes at 350 degrees or until baked through. Remove and set aside to cool completely.

6. Prepare the glaze. In a bowl, add in the powdered sugar and brewed coffee. Whisk until smooth in consistency. Spread over the top of the brownies.

7. Sprinkle the rainbow sprinkles over the top.

8. Slice into bars and serve immediately.

NUTRITION: Calorie: 160 kcal Fat: 6 g Carbs: 23 g Sodium: 80 mg Protein: 2g

119. Magic Brownie Bars

Preparation Time: 10 Minutes
Cooking Time: 55 Minutes
Servings: 12

INGREDIENTS

- 1 ½ cups of semi-sweet chocolate chips
- ½ cup of butter
- 1 cup of white sugar
- 2 eggs
- 1 egg yolk
- 1 cup of all-purpose flour
- ½ teaspoons of pure vanilla

Ingredients for the layers:

- 1 cup of chocolate chips
- 1 cup of butterscotch chips
- 1 cup of coconut, shredded
- 1, 14.5 ounce can of condensed sweetened milk

DIRECTION

1. Preheat the oven to 350 degrees.
2. In a bowl, add in the butter and semi-sweet chocolate chips. Microwave for 30 seconds or until melted. Stir well to mix.
3. In the bowl, add in the pure vanilla and eggs. Whisk well until mixed.
4. Add in the all-purpose flour and stir well until just mixed.
5. Pour into a greased baking dish.
6. Place into the oven to bake for 20 minutes.
7. Remove the brownies from the oven. Sprinkle the chocolate chips, butterscotch chips, shredded coconut and condensed milk over the top.
8. Place back into the oven to bake for 25 minutes.
9. Remove and set aside to cool completely.
10. Slice and serve.

NUTRITION: Calorie: 400 kcal Fat: 17 g Carbs: 59 g Sodium: 230 mg Protein: 4 g

120. Reese's Cheesecake Brownies

Preparation Time: 10 Minutes
Cooking Time: 30 Minutes
Servings: 12

INGREDIENTS:

- 1, 19.5-ounce box of chocolate fudge brownie mix
- 8 ounces of cream cheese, soft
- 1, 14 ounce can of condensed sweetened milk
- ½ cup of creamy peanut butter
- 12 ounces of Reese's pieces
- 1, 12-ounce bag of milk chocolate chips
- 3 Tablespoons of heavy whipping cream
- 12 Reese's peanut butter cups, chopped

DIRECTION

1. Preheat the oven to 350 degrees. Grease a baking dish with cooking spray.
2. Prepare the chocolate fudge brownie mix according to the directions on the package. Spread into a baking dish.
3. In a bowl, add in the cream cheese. Beat with an electric mixer until fluffy in consistency. Add in the condensed milk and creamy peanut butter. Continue to beat until smooth in consistency.
4. Add in the Reese's pieces. Fold gently to incorporate. Pour over the brownie layer in the baking dish.
5. Place into the oven to bake for 40 minutes or until baked through. Remove and set aside to cool for 30 minutes.
6. In a bowl, add in the heavy whipping cream and peanut butter cups. Microwave for 30 seconds to 1 minute or until melted. Stir well to mix. Spread over the top of the brownies.
7. Slice into bars and serve.

NUTRITION: Calorie: 588.7 kcal Fat: 33.4 g Carbs: 65.2 g Sodium: 291.7 Protein: 8.6 g

CHAPTER 4: ICE CREAM RECIPE

121. Hot Fudge Ice Cream Dessert

Preparation Time: 25 Minutes

Cooking Time: 25 Minutes

Servings: 6 servings.

INGREDIENTS:

- 1 cup miniature marshmallows
- 3/4 cup evaporated milk
- 1/2 cup semisweet chocolate chips
- 1/4 cup butterscotch chips
- 1/4 cup milk chocolate chips
- 10 vanilla wafers
- 1-quart butter pecan ice cream, softened
- 9 pecan halves, toasted
- 4 maraschino cherries

DIRECTIONS:

1. To make fudge sauce, mix together the marshmallows, milk and chips in a saucepan. Cook and stir on low heat till the mixture is smooth and melts. Take off from heat and refrigerate till chilled.

2. Use vanilla wafers to line a 6-inch springform pan's bottom. Add about 1 cup ice cream on top; press to form a smooth layer. Add a third of the fudge sauce on top. Freeze until set, for about 30 minutes. Redo these layers twice, freeze after each layer. Add pecans and cherries on top. Cover and freeze till firm. Take out of the freezer 10-15 minutes before serving.

NUTRITION: Calories: 501 calories Total Carbohydrate: 55 g Cholesterol: 46 mg Total Fat: 30 g Fiber: 1 g Protein: 8 g Sodium: 216 mg

122. Raspberry Hot Fudge Sundae

Preparation Time: 30 Minutes
Cooking Time: 30 Minutes
Servings: 6-8

INGREDIENTS:

- 1-1/2 cups frozen raspberries (without syrup)
- 1-quart vanilla ice cream, softened

Raspberry Sauce:

- 1 cup sugar
- 1/4 cup water
- 3 cups raspberries (without syrup)

Hot Fudge Sauce:

- 2/3 cup milk
- 1/4 cup butter
- 1/4 tsp. salt
- 2 cups (12 oz.) semisweet chocolate chips
- 1 tsp. vanilla extract

Whipped Almond Cream Topping:

- 1 cup heavy whipping cream
- 1 tsp. almond extract

DIRECTIONS:

1. Fold the raspberries into the vanilla ice cream gently; add into a covered freezer container and freeze till firm.
2. To make the raspberry sauce, add sugar and water into a 2 qt. saucepan; boil on medium heat for 1 minute. Take off heat; let it cool down for 15 minutes. Gently stir raspberries into the mix and refrigerate.
3. To make the fudge sauce, mix together salt, butter and milk in a double boiler's top over hot (not boiling) water.
4. Heat till the butter melts; add in the chocolate, stir till the chips melt and mixture is smooth. Take off heat and stir vanilla into the mix.
5. Right before serving, whip cream till it can hold soft peaks; fold almond extract into the cream. In large sundae dish or dessert bowl, add 2-3 tbsps. of each sauce on top of the ice-cream. Add a dollop of whipped topping on top to garnish.

NUTRITION: Calories: 633 calories Total Carbohydrate: 76 g Cholesterol: 88 mg Total Fat: 37 g
Fiber: 4 g Protein: 6 g Sodium: 212 mg

123. Homemade Peach Ice Cream

Preparation Time: 30 Minutes

Cooking Time: 0 Minutes

Servings: 2

INGREDIENTS

- 1 cup vanilla ice cream, softened

- 2/3 cup frozen unsweetened sliced peaches

- 1/8 tsp. vanilla extract

- Dash ground cinnamon

DIRECTION

1. In a blender, combine the peach, ice cream, cinnamon and vanilla; process, covered until smooth. In small freezer-safe dessert dishes, pour the mixture; freeze while covering until serving.

NUTRITION INFORMATION: Calories: 158 calories Total Carbohydrate: 22 g Cholesterol: 29 mg Total Fat: 7 g Fiber: 1 g Protein: 3 g Sodium: 53 mg

124. Easy Strawberry Cheesecake Ice Cream

Preparation Time: 15 Minutes

Cooking Time: 0 Minutes

Servings: 2

INGREDIENTS

- 1 cup half-and-half cream
- 1 tbsp. vanilla extract
- 2 tsps. grated lemon peel
- 2 tsps. lemon juice
- 1 cup sugar
- 1 package (8 oz.) cream cheese, cubed and softened
- 1 cup heavy whipping cream
- 1-1/2 cups fresh strawberries
- Sliced fresh strawberries or crushed graham crackers, optional

DIRECTION

1. In a blender, add the first 6 ingredients. Process, covered, until smooth. Put in the whipping cream. Process, covered, until blended. Transfer to the large bowl. Put one and a half cups of strawberries into blender. Process, covered, until pureed. Then stir into the cream mixture. Fill no more than 2/3 full the cylinder of the ice cream maker. Place the ice cream into freezer containers, letting the headspace expand. Freeze until firm, about 4 to 6 hours. Enjoy with graham crackers and sliced strawberries, if desired.

NUTRITION: Calories: 234 kcal Carbohydrate: 20 g Fat: 16 g Protein: 2 g Sodium: 87 mg

125. Homemade Strawberry Ice Cream

Preparation Time: 20 Minutes

Cooking Time: 0 Minutes

Servings: 2

INGREDIENTS

- 6 large egg yolks
- 2 cups whole milk
- 1 cup sugar
- 1/4 tsp. salt
- 1 tsp. vanilla extract
- 2 cups heavy whipping cream
- 2 cups crushed fresh strawberries, sweetened

DIRECTION

1. Put milk and egg yolks on top of the double boiler, then beat. Put in salt and sugar. Cook while stirring over the simmering water until the mixture coats the metal spoon and thickened. Let cool. Put in strawberries, vanilla and cream. Transfer to cylinder of an ice cream freezer. Place into the freezer container when the ice cream is frozen. Freeze for about 2 to 4 hours. Then enjoy!

NUTRITION: Calories: 265 kcal Carbohydrate: 22 g Fat: 19 g Protein: 4 g Sodium: 88 mg

126. Maple-Sweetened Ice Cream

Preparation Time: 1 Hour 45 Minutes
Cooking Time: 0 Minutes
Servings: 4

INGREDIENTS:

- 1 ½ cups each milk and heavy cream
- Seeds from 2 vanilla beans
- 4 egg yolks
- ½ cup cane sugar
- ¼ cup maple syrup
- 1 teaspoon vanilla extract
- ¼ teaspoon sea salt
- ½ cup walnuts, coarsely chopped

DIRECTIONS:

1. In a saucepan, combine together the milk, cream, and vanilla and bring to a simmer. Add the egg yolks and whisk briskly until combined. Add the sugar, maple syrup, vanilla extract, and salt until thickened. Chill the mixture in the fridge before adding the walnuts and transferring to the ice cream maker.

NUTRITION: Calories: 340 kcal Fat: 22g Sodium: 250mg Carbohydrate: 32g Protein: 8g

127. Honeyed Peaches Ice Cream

Preparation Time: 1 Hour
Cooking Time: 0 Minutes
Servings: 8

INGREDIENTS:

- 3 cups pitted peaches
- ¾ cup cane sugar
- 1 cup cream
- 2 egg yolks
- $^1/_3$ cup honey
- 1 tablespoon each cinnamon and vanilla extract
- ½ teaspoon sea salt

DIRECTIONS:

1. Puree the peaches in a blender and stir in the rest of the ingredients.
2. Pour mixture into ice cream maker and freeze according to instructions.

NUTRITION AL INFORMATION: Calories: 590 kcal Fat: 42g Sodium: 60mg Carbohydrate: 65g Protein: 8g

128.   Super-Quick Strawberry Ice Cream

Preparation Time: 10 Minutes
Cooking Time: 0 Minutes
Servings: 4

INGREDIENTS:

- 1 cup strawberries

- 2 bananas, peeled and frozen

- ½ teaspoon vanilla extract

- ¼ cup 2% milk

DIRECTIONS:

1. Combine all ingredients in the food processor until smooth.

2. Serve immediately or freeze until ready to serve.

NUTRITION: Calories: 370 kcal Fat: 25g Sodium: 30mg Carbohydrate: 38g Protein: 4g

129. Very Vanilla Ice Cream

Preparation Time: 1 Hour
Cooking Time: 0 Minutes
Servings: 6

INGREDIENTS:

- ¼ cup icing sugar

- ½ cup cane sugar

- 2 cups cream

- 1 tablespoon vanilla extract

- Seeds from 3 vanilla beans

- 1 teaspoon cinnamon

DIRECTIONS:

Combine all ingredients in a bowl and mix until well-combined. Pour into ice cream maker and freeze according to instructions.

NUTRITION: Calories: 300 kcal Fat: 28g Sodium: 35mg Carbohydrate: 22g Protein: 4g

130. Cherry Almond Ice Cream

Preparation Time: 1 Hour 15 Minutes
Cooking Time: 0 Minutes
Servings: 4

INGREDIENTS:

- 2 cups cream
- ½ cup cane sugar
- 1 cup pitted cherries
- 1 tablespoon lemon juice
- 1 ½ teaspoon almond extract
- ¼ cup slivered almonds

DIRECTIONS:

1. Puree the cherries in a blender.
2. Mix the cherries with the cream, sugar, lemon juice, and almond extract and stir until well-combined.
3. Stir the almonds in gently and place in ice cream maker; freeze according to manufacturer's instructions.

NUTRITION: Calories: 270 Fat: 18g Sodium: 240mg Carbohydrate: 42g Protein: 8g

131. Apple Raisin Ice Cream

Preparation Time: 40 Minutes
Cooking Time: 0 Minute
Servings: 6

INGREDIENTS:

- 2 cups cream
- 1 cup apples, chopped finely
- $^1/_3$ cup apple juice
- 1 tablespoon lemon juice
- 1 teaspoon cinnamon
- ¾ cup raisins

DIRECTIONS:

Mix together all ingredients until well-combined.

Pour into ice cream maker and freeze according to manufacturer's instructions.

NUTRITION: Calories: 340 Fat: 22g Sodium: 370mg Carbohydrate: 45g Protein: 8g

132. Chocolate Salted Ice Cream

Preparation Time: 2 Hours

Cooking Time: 0 Minutes

Servings: 6

INGREDIENTS:

- 1 cup cream

- ½ cup chocolate milk

- $^1/_3$ cup cane sugar

- 1 teaspoon vanilla extract

- 1 teaspoon sea salt

DIRECTIONS:

Mix together all ingredients in a bowl and stir until well-combined.

Freeze until ready to serve.

NUTRITION: Calories: 480 kcal Fat: 35g Sodium: 160mg

Carbohydrate: 31g Protein: 9g

133. Cookies and Cream

Preparation Time: 20 Minutes
Cooking Time: 0
Servings: 10

INGREDIENTS

Cookies crumbs

- 3/4 cup of almond flour
- 1/4 cup of cocoa powder
- 1/4 teaspoon of baking powder
- 1/4 cup of erythritol
- 1/2 teaspoon of vanilla extract
- 1 1/2 teaspoons of coconut oil, softened
- 1 egg
- Pinch of salt

Ice cream

- 2 1/2 cups of whipped cream
- 1 tablespoon of vanilla extract
- 1/2 cup of erythritol
- 1/2 cup of unsweetened almond milk

DIRECTIONS

1. Preheat the oven to 300 ° F. Line up a round 9-inch cake pan with parchment paper and spray with the oil of your choice. Add the almond flour, cocoa powder, baking soda, erythritol and salt in a medium bowl and mix until smooth. Add the vanilla extract and coconut oil and mix until the dough turns into crumbs. Add the egg and mix until the dough begins to stick and forms a ball. Place the dough in a separate cake pan and gently squeeze the dough with your fingers until it covers the bottom of the pan. Place the pan in the preheated oven and bake for 20 minutes or until the center of the cookie bounces back when pressed. When cooking is complete, remove the pan from the oven and allow it to cool. Allow the biscuit to cool and break it into small pieces. Mix whipped cream in a large bowl with an electric mixer. Add the vanilla extract and sweetener. Mix until well blended. Fill in the almond milk and mix until it thickens. Place the cream mixture in an ice cream maker and stir until mixture retains its shape. Slowly pour the crumbled biscuit into the ice cream maker. When all the biscuits have been mixed, place the ice

cream in a ½ liter container and freeze it at least 2 hours before serving.

NUTRITION: Calories 241 kcal Proteins 5 g Fats 30 g Carbs 5.1 g

134.   Chocolate Ice Cream

Preparation Time: 20 Minutes
Cooking Time: 0 Minutes
Servings: 5

INGREDIENTS

- ½ cup dark chocolate, broken into pieces
- ¼ cup of cocoa butter
- 4 big eggs, separated
- ¼ teaspoon of tartar
- ½ cup Erythritol or Swerve Powder
- 1 tablespoon of vanilla extract without sugar (15 ml)
- 1 ¼ cup thick cream or coconut cream

DIRECTIONS

1. Melt the chocolate and cocoa butter in a microwaveable bowl. Allow the melted chocolate to cool to room temperature. In the meantime, separate the egg whites from the yolk. Beat egg whites and tartar with an electric mixer. When the whites get thicker, slowly add the erythritol powder. Beat until they produce stiff peaks. Beat the cream in another bowl until soft peaks are obtained. In a third bowl, mix the egg yolks with the vanilla extract. Once the chocolate has cooled to room temperature, add about one third of the egg whites with a rubber spatula and mix with chocolate. Add the rest of the egg whites and fold gently without deflating. Stir in the egg yolk-vanilla mixture slowly. Add the whipped cream with a spatula and make a soft chocolate mousse. Transfer the chocolate mousse into a deep baking dish for at least 4 to 6 hours or until the mixture is ready.

NUTRITION: Calories 239 Proteins 3 g Fats 29.99 g Carbs 3.9

CHAPTER 5: PUDDING RECIPES

135. Homemade Caramel Custard Pudding

Preparation Time: 15 minutes
Cooking Time: 5 hours
Servings 10

INGREDIENTS

For the Caramel Sauce:

- 1/4 cup (60 ml) water
- 1 cup (220 g) light brown sugar

For the Custard:

- 8 (20 g) egg yolks
- 4 (60 g) whole eggs
- 1 (14.5 fl. oz. or 406 ml) can evaporated milk
- 1 (14 fl. oz. or 397 ml) can condensed milk
- 1 tsp. (5 ml) pure vanilla extract

DIRECTIONS

1. Combine water and sugar in a small pot or saucepan. Bring to a boil over medium-high heat. Lower heat to medium-low. Cook until the sugar caramelizes and becomes golden brown in color. Do not to overcook or else your caramel will taste bitter. Pour the caramel to the custard mold pans and spread evenly. Set aside. Fill your steamer with just enough amount of water and bring to a boil over medium heat. Meanwhile, combine together the yolks, eggs, sweetened condensed milk, evaporated milk, and vanilla extract in a large bowl. Stir gently until blended well. Strain the mixture into the prepared custard mold pans. Cover with foil and then put in the steamer. Run a knife along the sides of each custard to loosen them up. Invert onto serving plates. Serve and enjoy.

2. Note: Make sure to let it boil first before you put them in. Cover with lid. Reduce heat to low and steam until the custard is firm, about 40-45 minutes. Set aside to cool at room temperature, then refrigerate for at least 4 hours or until ready to serve.

NUTRITION: Calories - 280 kcal Fat - 0.0 g Carbohydrates - 37.2 g Protein - 9.3 g Sodium - 114 mg

136. Baked Custard Pudding with Maple

Preparation Time: 15 minutes
Cooking Time: 5 hours
Servings: 8

INGREDIENTS

For the Caramel Sauce:

1/4 cup (60 ml) water
3/4 cup (165 g) brown sugar
1/4 cup (60 g) maple syrup

For the Custard:

5 (60 g) whole eggs
8 (20 g) egg yolks
2 cups (500 ml) whole milk
1 can (14 fl. oz. or 397 ml) sweetened condensed milk
1 tsp. (5 ml) pure vanilla extract

DIRECTIONS

1. Preheat your oven and set it to 350 F (175).
2. Combine water, brown sugar, and 1/4 cup maple syrup in a saucepan. Bring to a boil over medium-high heat. Lower heat to medium-low. Cook until the sugar caramelizes and becomes golden brown in color. Pour into eight (3.5-ounce) ramekins and evenly spread the caramel. Set aside. Whisk together the eggs in a bowl until lightly beaten. Stir in whole milk, sweetened condensed milk, and vanilla extract until incorporated. Pour the custard mixture over caramel. Place the ramekins in a baking dish. Pour just enough water into the baking dish to cover ramekins halfway up the sides. Bake in the oven for about 40-45 minutes or until a skewer inserted in the center of the custard comes out clean. Remove from heat. Take out the ramekins from the baking dish and cool at room temperature. Chill for 4 hours before serving. Invert each ramekin onto individual plates.
3. Serve and enjoy.

NUTRITION: Calories- 297 kcal Fat - 9.8 g Carbohydrates - 44.1 g Protein - 9.1 g Sodium - 113 mg

137. Almond Caramel Custard

Preparation Time: 15 minutes
Total Time: 5 hours
Servings: 8

INGREDIENTS

- 1 cup (220 g) white sugar
- 1/4 cup (60 ml) water
- 5 (60 g) whole eggs
- 6 (20 g) egg yolks
- 2 tsp. (10 ml) almond extract
- thinly sliced banana, to serve (optional)
- chocolate shavings, to serve (optional)
- 1 (14.5 fl. oz. or 406 ml) can evaporated milk
- 1 (14 fl. oz. or 397 ml) can sweetened condensed milk

DIRECTIONS

1. Preheat your oven and set it to 350 F (175). In a heavy saucepan over medium heat, cook sugar with water until dissolved and golden brown. Pour into eight (3.5-ounce) flan molds or ramekins, tilting to coat the base. Set aside. In a large bowl, mix together the evaporated milk, condensed milk, eggs, and almond extract. Try not to incorporate any air into the custard mixture. Pour into prepared ramekins, and tap lightly on the counter to remove any bubbles. Place the ramekins inside a large baking dish. Fill the baking dish with boiling water to reach halfway up the sides of the flan molds. Bake in the oven until the middle of the flan is firm but still slightly jiggly when moved, about 45 minutes. Allow the custard to cool, then chill for 4 hours. To serve, run a knife around the sides to loosen the custard. Invert a plate on the mold, turn the mold over, and carefully unmold the custard with caramel syrup. Top with banana slices and chocolate shavings. Serve and enjoy.

NUTRITION: Calories- 338 kcal Fat - 12.9 g Carbohydrates - 45.0 g Protein - 11.7 g Sodium - 142 mg

138. Homemade Crème Brulee

Preparation Time: 10 minutes
Cooking Time: 5 hours
Servings 5

INGREDIENTS

- 6 (20 g) egg yolks
- 8 Tbsp. (110 g) granulated sugar, divided
- 1 tsp. (5 ml) pure vanilla extract
- 2 1/2 cups (375 ml) half and half cream
- 2 Tbsp. (30 g) brown sugar
- fresh blueberries, to serve
- mint leaves, for garnish

DIRECTIONS

1. Preheat your oven and set it to 350 F (175). In a medium pot or saucepan, mix together the egg yolks, 6 tablespoons of granulated sugar, and vanilla extract until blended well. Cook over a low flame, stirring constantly until almost boiling. Remove from heat. Stir in the cream. Mix well. Pour the cream mixture into the top part of a double boiler. Fill the bottom part with just enough water and bring to a simmer over medium flame, stirring constantly for 3-5 minutes. Remove mixture from the heat source and divide among five ramekins. Bake in the oven for about 40-45 minutes. Allow to cool at room temperature, then chill for 4 hours or until ready to serve. Combine the remaining white sugar and brown sugar in a small bowl and then sprinkle this mixture on top of each custard. With a kitchen blow torch, caramelize the sugar. Top with a few berries and garnish with mint leaves. Serve and enjoy.

NUTRITION: Calories- 325 kcal Fat - 19.4 g Carbohydrates - 32.9 g Protein - 7.0 g Sodium - 61 mg

139. Creamy Pudding with Raspberry Sauce

Preparation Time: 20 minutes
Cooking Time: 4 hours
Servings: 6

INGREDIENTS

- 2 cups (250 g) fresh raspberries, divided
- 3/4 cup (165 g) sugar, divided
- 1/3 cup (35 g) cornstarch
- 2 cups (500 ml) whole milk
- 1 cup (250 g) heavy cream

DIRECTIONS

1. Place 1 cup of raspberries in a food processor and puree. Pour into a small saucepan. Add 1/4 cup sugar and the remaining raspberries. Cook, stirring occasionally for about 8-10 minutes over medium flame. Remove from heat, and let cool. Cover and keep in the fridge until it's ready to use. In a separate saucepan, mix together the milk and cornstarch until dissolved. Cook over medium flame, stirring often until thickened. Stir in cream and the remaining 1/2 cup sugar. Heat for a few minutes until heated through, and the sugar has been dissolved completely. Pour among six ramekins, dividing the mixture evenly between them. Let cool, and then chill for at least 4 hours. Invert each mold onto individual serving plates. Top with prepared raspberry sauce. Serve and enjoy.

NUTRITION: Calories - 324 kcal Fat - 10.2 g Carbohydrates - 57.5 g Protein - 3.6 g Sodium - 42 mg

140. Banana Pudding Parfaits

Preparation Time: 15 Minutes

Cooking Time: 30 Minutes

Servings: 4

INGREDIENTS

- 24 vanilla wafers, divided
- 1 pkg. (3.4 oz.) JELL-O Banana Cream Flavor Instant Pudding
- 2 cups cold milk
- 3/4 cup thawed COOL WHIP Whipped Topping
- 1banana, cut into 20 slices

DIRECTION

1. Mash 20 wafers to make coarse crumbs. In a medium bowl, combine milk and pudding mix using a whisk for 2 minutes. Mix in COOL WHIP. Set aside 4 slices of banana for decorating. Then layer half of the wafer crumbs and the rest of bananas evenly in 4 dessert dishes; continue layering. Keep in the refrigerator for 15 minutes. Place the rest of the wafers and reserved banana slices on top just prior to serving.

NUTRITION: Calories: 320 kcal Carbohydrate: 55 g Fat: 9 g Protein: 6 g Sodium: 510 mg

141. Butterscotch Pudding Torte

Preparation Time: 15 Minutes

Cooking Time: 15 Minutes

Servings: 15

INGREDIENTS

- 1 package (16 oz.) cream-filled vanilla sandwich cookies, crushed
- 1/2 cup butter, melted
- 1 package (8 oz.) cream cheese, softened
- 1 cup confectioners' sugar
- 1 carton (12 oz.) frozen whipped topping, thawed, divided
- 2-1/2 cups cold 2% milk
- 2 packages (3.4 oz. each) instant butterscotch pudding mix

DIRECTION

1. For topping, put 1 cup cookie crumbs aside. Mix butter and leftover cookie crumbs in a small bowl; press into 13x9-in. greased dish. Beat confectioners' sugar and cream cheese till smooth in a big bowl; fold in 1 1/2 cups of whipped topping. Spread on crust. Whisk pudding mix and milk for 2 minutes in a small bowl; stand till soft set for 2 minutes. Put over the cream cheese layer. Put leftover whipped toppings over; sprinkle reserved crumbs. Cover; refrigerate for a minimum of 2 hours.

NUTRITION: Calories: 413 calories Carbohydrate: 49 g Fat: 22 g Protein: 4 g Sodium: 414 mg

142. Almond Bread Pudding

Preparation Time: 20 Minutes

Cooking Time: 55 Minutes

Servings: 15

INGREDIENTS

- 6 croissants
- 8 eggs
- 3 cups milk
- 2 cups sugar
- 2 tsps. vanilla extract
- 1 tsp. almond extract
- 1/4 cup almond paste, cut into small cubes
- 1/2 cup chopped almonds

STRAWBERRY CARAMEL SAUCE:

- 2 cups sugar
- 2 cups heavy whipping cream
- 1/2 cup frozen sweetened sliced strawberries, thawed

DIRECTION

1. Cut croissants to 1/2-in. pieces; put in 13x9-in. greased baking dish. Mix extracts, sugar, milk and eggs in big bowl; put on croissants. Stand for 10 minutes. Use almond paste to dot; sprinkle with almonds. The dish will become full. Bake for 35-40 minutes at 350° till inserted knife in middle exits clean. Meanwhile, mix and cook sugar with wooden spoon in heavy saucepan on medium heat for 20 minutes till it turns deep amber color and sugar melts. Put 1 cup cream in; it will bubble. Mix leftover cream in; cook till caramelized sugar melts completely for 10-15 minutes. Take off from heat; mix strawberries in. Serve with bread pudding.

NUTRITION: Calories: 531 kcal Carbohydrate: 72 g Fat: 24 g Protein: 9 g Sodium: 240 m

143. Apple Bread Pudding

Preparation Time: 20 Minutes

Cooking Time: 2 Hours 15 Minutes

Servings: 8

INGREDIENTS

- 1 (14 oz.) wide loaf French bread, crust removed and bread cut into 2x1-inch cubes
- 2 tbsps. butter
- 2 apples - peeled, quartered, cored, sliced crosswise into 1/4-inch thick pieces
- 1 cup muscovado or packed brown sugar, plus more for garnish
- 1/2 tsp. ground cinnamon
- 1/4 tsp. salt
- 4 large eggs
- 2 large egg yolks
- 3 cups milk
- 1 cup heavy cream
- 1 tsp. vanilla extract

DIRECTION

1. Preheat an oven to 165°C/325°F then grease 9x13-in. baking dish. On baking sheet, spread bread cubes; bake for about 20 minutes till crisp. Meanwhile, melt butter in skillet on medium heat; sauté apples for 7 minutes till tender. Put in prepped baking dish with bread then toss till combined. Whisk salt, cinnamon and sugar in big bowl; whisk yolks and whole eggs in till combined well. Whisk vanilla, cream and milk in; evenly put mixture on bread mixture. Stand for 45 minutes, covered, at room temperature. Preheat an oven to 165°C/325°F. Bake pudding for about 50 minutes till bread is set and absorbed custard.

NUTRITION: Calories: 420 kcal Carbohydrate: 46.8 g Fat: 20.2 g Protein: 13.4 g Sodium: 502 mg

CHAPTER 6: PIES AND TARTS

144. Banana Cheesecake Pie

Preparation Time: 25 Minutes

Cooking Time: 25 Minutes

Servings: 8

INGREDIENTS

- 1 package (11.1 oz.) no-bake home-style cheesecake mix
- 1/2 cup crushed vanilla wafers (about 15 wafers)
- 2 tbsps. sugar
- 1/2 cup cold butter, cubed
- 1 cup 2% milk plus 1-1/2 cups 2% milk, divided
- 1 package (3.4 oz.) instant banana cream pudding mix
- 2 medium bananas, cut into 1/4-in. slices
- 1 cup whipped topping
- 1/4 cup chopped pecans, toasted

DIRECTION

1. Combine sugar, wafers and contents of the crust mix in large bowl; cut in butter until coarse crumbs resemble. Press up sides and onto bottom of an unoiled 9 inches deep-dish pie plate. Beat contents of the filling mix and one cup of milk in large bowl on low speed until they are blended. Beat for 3 mins on medium, until they become smooth (the filling should become thick). Transfer to crust by spoon. Let chill for half an hour. In the meantime, whisk pudding mix and remaining milk in small bowl for 2 mins. Allow to stand until soft-set, about 2 mins (the pudding should become stiff). Place banana slices onto filling. Spread pudding over, followed by the whipped topping. Top with the pecans. Let chill at least 60 mins. Then serve.

NUTRITION: Calories: 468 kcal Carbohydrate: 64 g Fat: 22 g Protein: 5 g Sodium: 594 mg

145. Berry Cheesecake Pie

Preparation Time: 20 Minutes

Cooking Time: 55 Minutes

Servings: 8

INGREDIENTS

- 8 sheets phyllo dough (14 inches x 9 inches)
- 6 tbsps. butter, melted
- 2 packages (8 oz. each) cream cheese, softened
- 1/2 cup sugar
- 1 tsp. vanilla extract
- 2 eggs, lightly beaten
- 2 cups fresh or frozen blueberries
- 1/2 cup strawberry jelly
- 1 cup whipped topping
- Sliced fresh strawberries and additional blueberries, optional

DIRECTION

1. Arrange 1 phyllo sheet in a greased 9-inch pie plate; coat with butter. Repeat seven times; trim the edges. (Keep covering the remaining phyllo with plastic wrap and a damp towel to avoid drying out.) Bake at 425° for about 6 to 8 minutes, until edges look lightly browned (center would puff up). Let cool on a wire rack. To make the filling, beat vanilla, sugar, and cream cheese in a large bowl, until smooth. Add in eggs; whisk on low speed just until combined. Fold in blueberries. Spoon into crust. Bake at 350° for 10 minutes; to avoid over-browning, cover the edges with foil. Bake for an extra 23 to 27 minutes, until the center is almost set. Let cool on a wire rack for 1 hour. Put in the refrigerator until chilled. Beat the jelly in a small bowl until smooth; pour over the filling. Spread with the whipped topping. Garnish with extra blueberries and strawberries if desired.

NUTRITION: Calories: 466 kcal Carbohydrate: 41 g Fat: 31 g Protein: 7 g Sodium: 291 mg

146. Brownie Cheesecake Snickers Pie

Preparation Time: 45 Minutes

Cooking Time: 1 Hour 5 Minutes

Servings: 10

INGREDIENTS

- 1/3 cup butter, cubed
- 1 cup sugar
- 2 tbsps. water
- 6 oz. semisweet chocolate, chopped
- 1 tsp. vanilla extract
- 2 large eggs
- 3/4 cup all-purpose flour

Cream Cheese Layer:

- 10 oz. cream cheese, softened
- 1/3 cup sugar
- 1 large egg, beaten
- 1 tsp. vanilla extract
- 4 Snickers candy bars (2.07 oz. each), cut into 1/2-inch pieces
- 1/4 tsp. baking soda
- 1/8 tsp. salt

Glaze:

- 1/2 cup heavy whipping cream
- 4 oz. semisweet chocolate, chopped

DIRECTION

1. Set oven to preheat at 325°. Heat butter, sugar and water to in a heavy saucepan to a boil, stir continuously. Put off heat. Stir chocolate into the mixture until melted; let it cool down slightly. Stir vanilla into the mixture. Beat eggs in a large bowl until lightly beaten. Add chocolate mixture slowly; combine well. Combine salt, baking soda and flour; add into the egg mixture gradually. Spread it into a greased 9-in. deep-dish pie plate. Bake for 20 minutes. Let it cool down on a wire rack for S10 minutes. In the meantime, beat together vanilla, sugar, egg and cream cheese in

a large bowl until just blended. Layer candy bar pieces atop the brownie layer; spread the cream cheese mixture on top. Bake until top is set and edges are light brown for 18-20 minutes. Let it cool down on a wire rack for 1 hour. For glaze, heat cream till it simmers; put off heat. Add chocolate and stir till smooth. Let it cool down for 15 minutes; add on top of pie. Chill in the refrigerator until serving.

NUTRITION: Calories: 510 kcal Carbohydrate: 55 g Fat: 30 g Protein: 7 g Sodium: 246 mg

147. Caramel-pecan Cheesecake Pie

Preparation Time: 15 Minutes

Cooking Time: 50 Minutes

Servings: 8

INGREDIENTS

- 1 sheet refrigerated pie pastry
- 1 package (8 oz.) cream cheese, softened
- 1/2 cup sugar
- 4 large eggs
- 1 tsp. vanilla extract
- 1-1/4 cups chopped pecans
- 1 jar (12-1/4 oz.) fat-free caramel ice cream topping
- Additional fat-free caramel ice cream topping, optional

DIRECTION

1. Preheat the oven to 375 degrees. Place the pastry in a nine-inch deep-dish pie plate; trim the edges then flute. Whisk vanilla, cream cheese, one egg, and sugar together in a small bowl until smooth; spread the mixture into the pastry shell. Add pecans on top. Beat the remaining eggs in a small bowl; stir in caramel topping gradually until combined. Slowly transfer the mixture on top of the pecans. Bake pie for 35-40 minutes or until lightly browned. Cover the edges loosely with a foil after 20 minutes of baking if it browns too fast. Place on a wire rack to cool for an hour. Place in the refrigerator for 4 hours or overnight then slice. Add extra caramel ice cream topping to garnish if desired.

NUTRITION: Calories: 502 kcal Carbohydrate: 45 g Fat: 33 g Protein: 8 g Sodium: 277 mg

148. Cheesecake Cranberry Pie

Preparation Time: 15 Minutes

Cooking Time: 50 Minutes

Servings: 8

INGREDIENTS

- 2-1/2 cups whole-berry cranberry sauce
- 1 pastry shell (9 inches), baked
- 1 package (8 oz.) cream cheese, softened
- 2/3 cup sugar
- 2 eggs, lightly beaten
- 3 tbsps. all-purpose flour
- 1 tsp. vanilla extract

DIRECTION

1. Spread the pastry shell bottom with cranberry sauce. Beat sugar and cream cheese in small bowl until they become smooth. Beat in vanilla, flour and eggs on low speed until just combined. Add over the cranberry layer. Bake at for 35 to 40 mins 350°, until set at the middle. Place on wire rack to cool. Refrigerate, covered, at least 4 hours. Then cut to serve.

NUTRITION: Calories: 439 kcal Carbohydrate: 65 g Fat: 18 g Protein: 5 g Sodium: 219 mg

149. Chocolate Cheesecake Pie

Preparation Time: 30 Minutes

Cooking Time: 30 Minutes

Servings: 8

INGREDIENTS

- 1 package (8 oz.) cream cheese, softened
- 1/4 cup butter, softened
- 1/3 cup sugar
- 1-1/2 tsps. vanilla extract
- 1-1/2 cups milk chocolate chips, melted and cooled
- 1 carton (8 oz.) frozen whipped topping, thawed
- 1 graham cracker crust (9 inches)
- Chocolate curls, optional

DIRECTION

1. Blend vanilla, sugar, butter and cream cheese in a big bowl until forming a smooth mixture. Blend in cooled chocolate, Fold whipped topping into the mixture. Transfer to the pie shell. Chill in the refrigerator before serving. Add chocolate curls to decorate as you like.

NUTRITION: Calories: 535 kcal Carbohydrate: 48 g Fat: 35 g Protein: 6 g Sodium: 270 mg

150. Holiday Cheesecake Pie

Preparation Time: 30 Minutes

Cooking Time: 1 Hour 30 Minutes

Servings: 16

INGREDIENTS

- 1 can (15 oz.) solid-pack pumpkin
- 1 can (12 oz.) evaporated milk
- 3/4 cup sugar
- 4 oz. cream cheese, softened
- 1/2 tsp. pumpkin pie spice
- 1/4 tsp. salt
- 2 eggs, lightly beaten
- 2 graham cracker crusts (9 inches)
- 1-1/2 cups cold eggnog
- 1 package (3.4 oz.) instant vanilla pudding mix
- 1 cup whipped topping
- Additional whipped topping, optional

DIRECTION

1. Whisk salt, pumpkin pie spice, cream cheese, sugar, milk, and pumpkin together in a big bowl. Add eggs, whisk on low speed until just blended. Evenly distribute among the graham cracker crusts. Bake at 350° until a knife will come out clean when you insert it into the middle, about 45-55 minutes. Put on a wire rack to cool. Beat pudding mix and eggnog in a small bowl for 2 minutes. Fold in whipped topping. Spread onto the pies. Put a cover on and chill for 60 minutes. Use more whipped topping to garnish if you want.

NUTRITION: Calories: 266 kcal Carbohydrate: 37 g Fat: 11 g Protein: 5 gSodium: 297 mg

151. Apple Graham Pie

Preparation Time: 30 Minutes

Cooking Time: 30 Minutes

Servings: 8

INGREDIENTS

- 2 cups graham cracker crumbs
- 3/4 cup sugar, divided
- 1/2 cup butter, melted
- 4 cups sliced peeled tart apples (about 4 medium)
- 1 tsp. ground cinnamon

DIRECTION

1. Mix together butter, 1/4 cup of sugar and cracker crumbs until it crumbles in a bowl. Prepare an ungreased microwave-safe 9-in. pie plate and press 2/3 of the mixture so that it covers the bottom and the sides of the plate. Reserve the rest of the mixture.

2. Combine apples with the remaining sugar and cinnamon in a bowl; stir to coat. Put it onto the crust; use the reserved crumbs to sprinkle on top. Put into the microwave for 6 minutes on high heat without cover; rotate meanwhile. Continue to cook until the apples are softened or for 5-6 minutes longer. Let it cool on wire rack. Put into the refrigerator to store.

NUTRITION: Calories: 294 kcal Carbohydrate: 43 g Fat: 14 g Protein: 2 g Sodium: 243 mg

152. Caramel Toffee Ice Cream Pie

Preparation Time: 15 Minutes

Cooking Time: 25 Minutes

Servings: 8

INGREDIENTS

- 1-1/2 cups chocolate graham cracker crumbs (about 8 whole crackers)

- 2 tbsps. sugar

- 1 egg white, beaten

- 2 tbsps. butter, melted

- 4 cups fat-free vanilla frozen yogurt, softened, divided

- 2 English toffee candy bars (1.4 oz. each), coarsely chopped, divided

- 1/2 cup caramel ice cream topping, divided

DIRECTION

1. Preheat your oven to 375°. Mix sugar and cracker crumbs in a small bowl. Mix butter and egg white in. Up the sides and bottom of the 9-in. pie plate that's been coated using cooking spray, press on. Bake till set for 6-8 minutes. On a wire rack, completely cool.

2. Into crust, spread 2-2/3 cup frozen yogurt. Sprinkle 1/2 toffee bits on. Drizzle 1/2 caramel. Use caramel topping, toffee and leftover yogurt to layer. Cover. Freeze for 8 hours-overnight. Take out of the freezer 15 minutes prior to serving.

NUTRITION: Calories: 304 kcal Carbohydrate: 54 g Fat: 8 g Protein: 7 g Sodium: 289 mg

153. Cherry Mallow Dessert

Preparation Time: 25 Minutes

Cooking Time: 25 Minutes

Servings: 9

INGREDIENTS

- 1-1/2 cups graham cracker crumbs
- 1/3 cup butter, melted
- 1 can (21 oz.) cherry pie filling
- 3 cups miniature marshmallows
- 1 cup heavy whipping cream, whipped

DIRECTION

1. Reserve a tbsp. of graham cracker crumbs to use as topping. Put the rest of crumbs in a bowl; mix in butter until combined. Press the mixture into a 9-inch square baking pan coated with grease. Put in an oven and bake at 350° until light brown, about 10-12 minutes. Let cool completely. Spread the pie filling over crust. Fold marshmallows into the whipped cream; spread on the filling. Scatter with the reserved crumbs. Put in refrigerator for at least 6 hours.

NUTRITION: Calories: 339 kcal Carbohydrate: 44 g Fat: 18 g Protein: 2 g Sodium: 183 mg

CHAPTER 7: FRUITS DESSERT

154.   Fresh Apple Cobbler

Preparation Time: 30 Minutes

Cooking Time: 30 Minutes

Servings: 6

INGREDIENTS

- 1/2 cup all-purpose flour
- 2 tbs. unsalted butter
- 2 tbs. cold water
- 1 tbs. cornstarch
- 1/2 cup apple juice
- 5 cups apples, peeled, sliced and cored
- 1/3 cup light brown sugar
- 1/2 tsp. ground cinnamon
- 1/4 tsp. ground nutmeg
- 1/4 tsp. ground cloves

DIRECTIONS

1. In a small bowl, add the all-purpose flour and butter. Using a pastry blender, cut the butter into the flour until you have coarse crumbs. Add one tablespoon water to the bowl. Using a fork, mix until the dough is moistened. Add the remaining water if needed to form a soft but firm dough. Shape the dough into a ball and wrap the dough in plastic wrap. Chill the dough for 15 minutes. In a small bowl, stir together the cornstarch and 1/4 cup apple juice. In a sauce pan over medium heat, add 1/4 cup apple juice, apples, brown sugar, cinnamon, nutmeg and cloves. Stir constantly and bring the apples to a boil. When the apples are boiling, reduce the heat to low. Stir occasionally and simmer the apples for 10 minutes. Stir in the cornstarch mixture and cook until the filling thickens and bubbles. Remove the pan from the heat. Spray an 8" square baking dish with non-stick cooking spray. Spoon the filling into the prepared pan. Roll the

dough into an 8" square between two sheets of waxed paper. Place the dough in the freezer for 5 minutes. Remove the dough from the freezer and remove the top sheet of waxed paper from the dough. Cut the dough into 1/2" strips and place the strips over the filling in the dish to form a lattice design. Preheat the oven to 425°. Bake for 30 minutes or until the crust is golden brown and the filling bubbly. Remove the cobbler from the oven and cool for 5 minutes before serving.

NUTRITION: Calorie: 192.4 kcal Fat: 6.3 g Carbs: 36.6 g Sodium: 46.6 mg Protein: 1.8 g

155. Peachy Blueberry Cobbler

Preparation Time: 10 Minutes

Cooking Time: 50 Minutes

Servings: 8

INGREDIENTS

- 3 peaches, peeled and sliced
- 1 cup plus 2 tbs. granulated sugar
- 1 cup all-purpose flour
- 2 tsp. baking powder
- 1 tsp. salt
- 1 cup whole milk
- 1/2 cup unsalted butter, melted
- 2/3 cup fresh or thawed frozen blueberries

DIRECTIONS

1. In a small bowl, add the peaches and 2 tablespoons granulated sugar. Toss until the peaches are coated in the sugar. Preheat the oven to 350°. Spray a 12 x 8 x 2 baking dish with non-stick cooking spray. In a mixing bowl, add 1 cup granulated sugar, all-purpose flour, baking powder and salt. Stir until combined. Add the milk and butter to the dry ingredients. Stir until well combined and pour the batter into the baking dish. Arrange the peaches over the batter. Sprinkle the blueberries over the batter. Bake for 50 minutes or until the batter rises to the top and the cobbler is golden brown. Remove the cobbler from the oven and cool for 5 minutes before serving.

NUTRITION: Calorie:182 kcal Fat: 3 g Carbs: 38 g Sodium: 357.4 mg Protein: 4.4 g

156. Easy Fresh Cherry Cobbler

Preparation Time: 10 Minutes

Cooking Time: 35 Minutes

Servings: 8

INGREDIENTS

- 1/2 cup unsalted butter
- 1 cup self-rising flour
- 1 cup granulated sugar
- 1 cup whole milk
- 1/2 tsp. almond extract
- 4 cups fresh cherries, pitted

DIRECTIONS

1. Preheat the oven to 375°. Add the butter to a 12 x 8 x 2 baking dish. Place the dish in the oven until the butter melts. In a mixing bowl, add the self-rising flour, granulated sugar, milk and almond extract. Whisk until well blended. Pour the batter over the melted butter in the baking dish. Spoon the cherries over the batter. Bake for 35 minutes or until the crust is golden brown. Remove the cobbler from the oven and cool for 5 minutes before serving.

NUTRITION: Calorie: 170.6 kcal Fat: 34. G Carbs: 34.3 g Sodium: 100.1 mg Protein: 2.8 g

157. Fresh Blueberry Crisp

Preparation Time: 5 Minutes

Cooking Time: 45 Minutes

Servings: 6

INGREDIENTS

- 4 cups fresh blueberries
- 1 cup light brown sugar
- 3/4 cup all-purpose flour
- 3/4 cup old fashioned oats
- 1/2 cup melted unsalted butter

DIRECTIONS

1. Preheat the oven to 350°. Spread the blueberries in a 2-quart baking dish. In a mixing bowl, add the brown sugar, all-purpose flour, oats and butter. Stir until combined and sprinkle over the blueberries. Bake for 45 minutes. Remove the crisp from the oven and cool for 10 minutes before serving. Serve with whipped cream or ice cream if desired.

NUTRITION: Calorie: 136.4 kcal Fat: 5.2 g Carbs: 24.3 g Sodium: 29.2 mg Protein: 2.5 g

158. Blackberry Almond Cobbler

Preparation Time: 30 Minutes
Cooking Time: 35 Minutes
Servings: 6

INGREDIENTS

- 1 cup all-purpose flour
- 1/3 cup ground almonds
- 1 tbs. powdered sugar
- 1/4 cup plus 3 tbs. unsalted butter
- 3 cups fresh blackberries
- 1 cup water
- 1 cup plus 1 tbs. granulated sugar

DIRECTIONS

1. In a mixing bowl, add the all-purpose flour, almonds and powdered sugar. Stir until well combined. Add 1/4 cup plus 1 tablespoon butter to the bowl. Using a pastry blender, cut the butter into the dry ingredients until you have coarse crumbs. Refrigerate the dough for 15 minutes. In a sauce pan over medium heat, add 2 tablespoons butter, blackberries, water and 1 cup granulated sugar. Stir constantly and bring the blackberries to a boil. When the blackberries are boiling, remove the pan from the heat. Preheat the oven to 375°. Spray a 2-quart casserole dish with non-stick cooking spray. Pour the blackberries into the casserole dish. Lightly flour your work surface. Remove the dough from the refrigerator and place the dough on your work surface. Knead the dough for a couple of minutes or until the dough is smooth. Roll the dough out to fit your casserole dish. Place the dough over the blackberries and attach the dough to the edges of the dish. Brush the crust lightly with water. Sprinkle 1 tablespoon granulated sugar over the crust. Using a sharp knife, cut several small slits in the top of the crust. Bake for 35 minutes or until the crust is done, golden brown and the filling bubbly. Remove the cobbler from the oven and cool for 10 minutes before serving.

NUTRITION: Calorie: 276 kcal Fat: 12.2 g Carbs: 38 g Sodium: 183 mg Protein: 5.6 g

159. Raspberry Crisp

Preparation Time: 10 Minutes

Cooking Time: 25 Minutes

Servings: 8

INGREDIENTS

- 4 cups fresh raspberries
- 3/4 cup granulated sugar
- 2 tbs. cornstarch
- 1 3/4 cups quick cooking oats
- 1 cup all-purpose flour
- 1 cup light brown sugar
- 1/2 tsp. baking soda
- 1/2 cup cold unsalted butter

DIRECTIONS

Preheat the oven to 350°. Crush 1 cup raspberries. Add cold water to the raspberries to measure 1 cup total. In a sauce pan over medium heat, add the granulated sugar and cornstarch. Stir until combined and add the one cup crushed raspberries and water. Stir constantly and bring the raspberries to a boil. Boil for 2 minutes or until the raspberries thicken. Remove the pan from the heat and stir in 3 cups raspberries. Spray a 9" square baking pan with non-stick cooking spray. Spoon the raspberries into the dish. In a mixing bowl, add the oats, all-purpose flour, brown sugar and baking soda. Stir until combined. Add the butter to the bowl. Using a fork, cut the butter into the dry ingredients until you have coarse crumbs. Sprinkle the crumbs over the top of the raspberries. Bake for 25 minutes or until the crisp is bubbly and the topping golden brown. Remove the crisp from the oven and cool for 15 minutes before serving.

NUTRITION: Calorie: 65.7 kcal Fat: 2.3 g Carbs: 11.2 g Sodium: 17.5 mg Protein: 0.7 g

160. Strawberry Cookie Tarts

Preparation Time: 20 Minutes

Cooking Time: 10 Minutes

Servings: 12

INGREDIENTS

- 1/3 cup vegetable shortening
- 1/3 cup granulated sugar
- 1 egg
- 1 tsp. vanilla extract
- 1 cup all-purpose flour
- 1 tsp. baking powder
- 1/2 tsp. salt
- 1 egg white, beaten until foamy
- 1/4 cup red currant jelly
- 2 tsp. water
- 1-pint fresh strawberries, sliced

DIRECTIONS

1. In a mixing bowl, add the vegetable shortening and granulated sugar. Using a mixer on medium speed, beat for 2 minutes or until light and fluffy. Add the egg and vanilla extract to the bowl. Mix for 2 minutes or until well combined. Add the all-purpose flour, baking powder and salt. Mix only until combined. Turn the mixer off and form the dough into a ball. Wrap the dough in plastic wrap and refrigerate until well chilled. You do not want to add any extra flour to the dough. Roll the dough in a circle about 1/8" thick between two sheets of waxed paper.

Using a 4" round cutter, cut out 12 cookies. Roll the dough scraps to cut out all the cookies. Line a baking sheet with waxed paper. Place the cookies on the waxed paper and freeze for 15 minutes. Preheat the oven to 375°. Spray a cookie sheet with non-stick cooking spray. Place the cookies on the baking sheet. Brush the cookies with the beaten egg white. Bake for 10-12 minutes or until the cookies are lightly browned. In a small sauce pan over low heat, add the currant jelly and water. Stir until the jelly melts and remove the pan from the heat. Cool the jelly for 5 minutes. Brush one side of the cookies with half the jelly. Place the strawberries over the cookies. Brush the remaining jelly over the strawberries before serving.

NUTRITION: Calorie: 160 kcal Fat: 10 g Carbs: 16 g Sodium: 140 mg Protein: 2 g

161.   Blackberry Flan Tart

Preparation Time: 15 Minutes
Cooking Time: 20 Minutes
Servings: 8

INGREDIENTS

- 1/3 cup plus 1 tbs. unsalted butter, softened
- 1 2/3 cups granulated sugar
- 3 egg yolks
- 1/3 cup whole milk
- 1 1/4 cups all-purpose flour
- 1/2 tsp. salt
- 1/2 tsp. baking soda
- 1 tsp. cream of tartar
- 1/2 tsp. almond extract
- 1/2 tsp. ground allspice
- 3 cups fresh blackberries or thawed frozen blackberries
- 2 cups chilled whipped cream

DIRECTIONS

1. Spray a 10" tart or flan pan with non-stick cooking spray. In a mixing bowl, add 1/3 cup butter and 2/3 cup granulated sugar. Using a mixer on medium speed, beat until the mixture is light and fluffy. Add the egg yolks and milk to the bowl. Beat for 3 minutes or until the batter is creamy. Add 1 cup all-purpose flour, 1/4 teaspoon salt, baking soda, cream of tartar and almond extract. Mix until the batter is combined. Preheat the oven to 350°. Spoon the batter into the prepared pan making certain all the pan is covered. Bake for 20 minutes or until lightly browned. Remove the pan from the oven and cool completely before filling. For the filling, add 1/4 cup all-purpose flour, 1 cup granulated sugar, 1/4 teaspoon salt and allspice to a sauce pan over low heat. Stir until combined and add the blackberries. Stir constantly and cook for 2 minutes. Add 1 tablespoon butter and cook until the mixture thickens. Remove the pan from the heat and cool the filling before using. When ready to serve, spoon the filling into the cooled crust. Spread the chilled whipped cream over the top and serve.

NUTRITION: Calorie: 322 kcal Fat: 16.57 g Carbs: 43.28 g Sodium: 330 mg Protein: 3.67 g

CHAPTER 8: CANDIES AND CHOCOLATES

162. Almond Coconut Candies

Preparation Time: 25 Minutes

Cooking Time: 25 Minutes

Servings: 60

INGREDIENTS

- 4-1/2 cups confectioners' sugar
- 3 cups sweetened shredded coconut
- 1 cup sweetened condensed milk
- 1/2 cup butter, melted
- 1 tsp. vanilla extract
- 60 whole unblanched almonds

FROSTING:

- 1-1/2 cups confectioners' sugar
- 1/2 cup baking cocoa
- 1/2 cup butter, melted
- 3 tbsps. hot coffee

DIRECTION

1. Mix the first 5 ingredients together in a large mixing bowl. Form mixture into balls about 1 inch; arrange balls on lightly greased baking sheets. Pat an almond on top of each ball. Refrigerate for 60 minutes. Mix frosting ingredients together until no lumps remain; instantly frost over the candies. Refrigerate until frosting is solid. Keep chilled in the fridge.

NUTRITION: Calories: 123 kcal Carbohydrate: 18 g Fat: 6 g Protein: 1 g Sodium: 50 mg

163. Angel Food Candy

Preparation Time: 20 Minutes

Cooking Time: 1 Hour 15 Minutes

Servings: 30

INGREDIENTS

- 1 cup white sugar
- 1 cup dark corn syrup
- 1 tbsp. vinegar
- 1 tbsp. baking soda
- 1 lb. chocolate confectioners' coating

DIRECTION

1. Butter a 9x13 inch baking dish. Mix vinegar, corn syrup and sugar over medium heat in a medium saucepan. Cook while stirring until sugar is dissolved. Without stirring, heat to 300-310°F (149- 154°C), or until when you drop a small amount of syrup into cold water, it forms hard, brittle threads. Take out of the heat; stir in baking soda. Transfer into buttered pan; do not spread. (Mixture should not fill the pan). Let cool completely. Melt coating chocolate while stirring frequently until smooth over a double boiler or in a microwave. Break cooled candy into bite-sized pieces and coat with melted candy coating. Allow to set on waxed paper. Keep covered tightly.

NUTRITION: Calories: 129 kcal Carbohydrate: 22.2 g Fat: 6 g Protein: 1.2 g Sodium: 135 mg

164. Austrian Chocolate Balls

Preparation Time: 15 Minutes

Cooking Time: 45 Minutes

Servings: 42

INGREDIENTS

- 2 (1 oz.) squares unsweetened chocolate
- 1/3 cup butter
- 1 cup white sugar
- 1 egg
- 1 egg yolk
- 1/2 tsp. almond extract
- 1 1/3 cups all-purpose flour
- 1/2 cup finely chopped walnuts
- 1 (1 oz.) square unsweetened chocolate
- 1 tbsp. butter
- 1/4 tsp. vanilla extract
- 1 cup confectioners' sugar
- 3 tbsps. Milk

DIRECTION

1. Melt 1/3 cup butter and 2 squares of chocolate over low heat in a small saucepan. Whisk constantly until melted; turn off the heat, and put to one side to cool. Turn oven to 350°F (175°C) to preheat. Combine egg and egg yolk in a medium bowl together with almond extract and sugar until fluffy and light. Mix in melted chocolate. Combine walnuts and flour; mix into the batter just until incorporated. Form dough into 3/4-inch balls, and arrange them 1 inch apart on unbuttered cookie sheets. If the dough feels too sticky, chill for half an hour before making balls. Bake for 8 to 12 minutes in the preheated oven until firm to the touch. Immediately remove to wire racks, and put aside to allow to cool. Melt 1 tbsp. butter and 1 square of chocolate together over low heat in a small saucepan, whisking often until no lumps remain. Put off the heat, and whisk in confectioners' sugar and vanilla until incorporated. Beat in milk, 1 tbsp. at a time, until glaze reaches desired thickness. Immerse top of the cookies into the glaze; let dry entirely before putting into an airtight container to store.

NUTRITION: Calories: 82 kcal; Carbs: 11.5 g Fat: 4 g Protein: 1.1 g Sodium: 15 mg

165. Banana Cream Chocolate Truffles

Preparation Time: 35 Minutes

Cooking Time: 35 Minutes

Servings: 48

INGREDIENTS

- 1 package (14.3 oz.) Golden Oreo cookies
- 1 package (8 oz.) cream cheese, softened
- 2 tsps. banana extract
- 1/3 cup mashed ripe banana
- 1 lb. milk chocolate candy coating, melted
- Dried banana chips, coarsely crushed

DIRECTION

1. In a food processor, blend cookies into fine crumbs. Beat cream cheese with extract in a mixing bowl until incorporated. Whisk in banana. Mix in cookie crumbs. Cover and freeze, about 2 hours, until solid enough to shape. Form mixture into balls about 1 inch. Immerse the balls in candy coating; arrange coated candies on baking sheets lined with waxed paper. Instantly sprinkle top with banana chips. Chill for about half an hour until firm. Keep chilled in a covered container in the fridge.

NUTRITION: Calories: 110 kcal Carbs: 13 g Fat: 6 g Protein: 1 g Sodium: 45 mg

166. Basic Truffles

Preparation Time: 10 Minutes

Cooking Time: 1 Hour 50 Minutes

Servings: 35

INGREDIENTS

- 12 oz. bittersweet chocolate, chopped
- 1/3 cup heavy cream
- 1 tsp. vanilla extract

DIRECTION

1. Mix together the cream and chocolate in a medium saucepan on medium heat. Let it cook and stir until the mixture becomes smooth and the chocolate melts. Take it out of the heat and whisk in the flavoring. Pour it into a small dish and let it chill in the fridge for 1 1/2 to 2 hours until it becomes set, yet not hard. Form it into balls and roll it in the toppings or use it to fill the candies.

NUTRITION: Calories: 62 kcal Carbohydrate: 5.6 g Fat: 4.1 g Protein: 0.7 g Sodium: 1 mg

167. Bittersweet Double Chocolate Truffles

Preparation Time: 30 Minutes

Cooking Time: 30 Minutes

Servings: 18

INGREDIENTS

- 1 cup 60% cacao bittersweet chocolate baking chips
- 3/4 cup whipped topping
- 1/4 tsp. ground cinnamon
- 1 cup milk chocolate chips
- 1 tsp. shortening
- Optional toppings: crushed peppermint candies, sprinkles and chopped nuts

DIRECTION

1. Heat bittersweet chips in a small saucepan over low heat until melted. Pour into a bowl and allow to cool for about 7 minutes until lukewarm. Beat cinnamon and whipped topping into the mixture. Freeze until firm enough to shape into balls, 15 minutes. Form into balls of an inch. Microwave shortening and milk chocolate chips until melted; stir until the mixture is smooth. Dunk truffles in chocolate and put on baking sheets lined with waxed paper. Add a sprinkle of preferred toppings immediately. Chill in the refrigerator to firm up. Keep refrigerated in an airtight container to store.

NUTRITION: Calories: 105 kcal Carbs: 12 g Fat: 6 g Protein: 1 g Sodium: 8 mg

168. Blueberry, Coconut, And Pistachio Chocolate Bark

Preparation Time: 10 Minutes; Cooking Time: 57 Minutes

Servings: 8

INGREDIENTS

3 (4 oz.) bars dark chocolate, chopped, divided

- 3 tbsps. shelled unsalted pistachios, coarsely chopped
- 3 tbsps. dried blueberries
- 1 tbsp. coconut chips
- 2 tsps. grated orange zest (optional)

DIRECTION

1. Microwave 8 oz. chocolate in a microwaveable ceramic or glass bowl for 1-3 minutes, stirring every 15 seconds. When chocolate is almost melted with chunks remaining still, take out of the microwave and mix until fully smooth. Put in the rest of 4 oz. unmelted chocolate. Whisk thoroughly until chocolate is completely melted. On a flat work surface, spread out a big piece of parchment paper. Transfer melted chocolate to parchment paper and use a spatula to thinly spread out into an even layer. Before the chocolate sets, quickly sprinkle orange zest, coconut chips, dried blueberries and pistachios on top. Allow to sit for 45 minutes until completely set. Beak into uneven pieces and keep in a tightly sealed container to store.

NUTRITION: Calories: 255 Carbs: 28.6 g Fat: 15.5 g Protein: 3.1 g Sodium: 4 mg

169. Caramel Pretzel Bites

Preparation Time: 20 Minutes
Cooking Time: 45 Minutes
Servings: 72

INGREDIENTS

- 2 tsps. butter, softened
- 4 cups pretzel sticks
- 2-1/2 cups pecan halves, toasted
- 2-1/4 cups packed brown sugar
- 1 cup butter, cubed
- 1 cup corn syrup
- 1 can (14 oz.) sweetened condensed milk
- 1/8 tsp. salt
- 1 tsp. vanilla extract
- 1 package (11-1/2 oz.) milk chocolate chips
- 1 tbsp. plus 1 tsp. shortening, divided
- 1/3 cup white baking chips

DIRECTION

1. Use foil to line a 13x9 in. pan; use softened butter to grease foil. Spread pecans and pretzels on bottom of the prepared pan. Mix salt, milk, corn syrup, butter cubes, brown sugar in a large heavy saucepan; cook and stir on medium heat till a candy thermometer reaches 240 degrees (it's the soft ball stage). Get the pan off heat. Put in vanilla and stir. Transfer the mixture onto the pretzel mixture. Put a tbsp. of shortening and chocolate chips together and melt in a microwave; stir till the mixture becomes smooth. Spread over the caramel layer. Melt the rest of shortening and white baking chips in the microwave; stir till the mixture becomes smooth. Drizzle over top. Allow to sit till the mixture is set. Lift candy out of pan by foil; get rid of foil. Butter a knife and use the knife to chop candy to bite sized pieces.

NUTRITION: Calories: 146 kcal Carbs: 19 g Fat: 8 g Protein: 1 g Sodium: 76 mg

170. Cherry Chocolate Bark

Preparation Time: 5 Minutes

Cooking Time: 40 Minutes

Servings: 18

INGREDIENTS

- 1 (12 oz.) bag semisweet chocolate chips
- 12 cherry-flavored candy canes, crushed
- 1/3 cup red confectioner's coating (optional)

DIRECTION

1. Line aluminum foil on 9x13-in. baking pan. Melt chocolate chips in microwave-safe ceramic/glass bowl for 1-3 minutes, varies on microwave, in 30-second intervals, mixing after every melting, till smooth. Don't overheat; chocolate will scorch. Spread melted chocolate quickly and evenly using a spatula in the prepared pan till its bottom is covered. Evenly drizzle the crushed candy on chocolate; lightly pat using clean spatula to help candy settle into chocolate. If using, melt red confectioners' coating in microwave-safe ceramic/glass bowl for 1-3 minutes, varies on microwave, in 30-second intervals, mixing after every melting. Put melted coating in resealable plastic bag; snip very small corner of bag off; use to drizzle bark with coating. Put pan in fridge/freezer for 30 minutes till hard. Remove from pan; peel foil off. Break to small pieces to serve.

NUTRITION: Calories: 180 kcal Carbs: 31.9 g Fat: 6.6 g Protein: 1 g Sodium: 12 mg

171. Chewy Chocolate Candies

Preparation Time: 45 Minutes

Cooking Time: 45 Minutes

Servings: 25

INGREDIENTS

- 2 tbsps. butter, melted
- 2 (1 oz.) squares unsweetened chocolate, melted and cooled
- 1/2 cup light corn syrup
- 3 cups confectioners' sugar, divided
- 3/4 cup powdered milk
- 1 tsp. vanilla extract

DIRECTION

1. Stir the chocolate and butter together in a medium mixing bowl. Beat in the vanilla, powdered milk, 2 cups of confectioner's sugar and corn syrup. The dough will get stiff. Sprinkle the leftover 1 cup of confectioner's sugar on a work surface, then transfer the dough onto the work surface and knead it until the leftover sugar is combined. Form it into small logs and wrap it using waxed paper.

NUTRITION INFORMATION: Calories: 107 kcal Carbohydrate: 21.9 g Fat: 2.1 g Protein: 1.6 g Sodium: 31 mg

172. Chocolate Almond Brittle

Preparation Time: 15 Minutes

Cooking Time: 15 Minutes

Servings: 1 lb.

INGREDIENTS

- 1 cup sugar
- 1/2 cup light corn syrup
- 1/8 tsp. salt
- 1 cup coarsely chopped almonds
- 1 tbsp. butter
- 1 tsp. vanilla extract
- 1-1/2 tsps. baking soda
- 3/4 lb. dark or milk chocolate candy coating

DIRECTION

1. Mix together salt, corn syrup and sugar in a 1 1/2-quart microwaveable bowl. Heat on high in the microwave without covering for 2 1/2 minutes. Mix in almonds; microwave on high for 2 1/2 minutes. Pour in vanilla and butter; microwave on high for a minute. Mix in baking soda. Once the mixture is frothy, immediately transfer to a greased metal baking sheet. Wait until fully cool. Break apart into 2-in pieces. Microwave chocolate until melted. Plunge one side of brittle in chocolate, then put onto waxed paper to harden. Keep in a tightly sealed container to store.

NUTRITION: Calories: 483 kcal Carbohydrate: 73 g Fat: 22 g Protein: 4 g Sodium: 313 mg

CHAPTER 9: DEEP-FRIED DESSERT

173. Apple Fritters

Preparation Time: 25 Minutes

Cooking Time: 30 Minutes

Servings: 20

INGREDIENTS

- 2 cups all-purpose flour
- 1/4 cup white sugar
- 1 tbsp. baking powder
- 1/2 tsp. ground nutmeg
- 1 tsp. salt
- 2 eggs
- 1 cup milk
- 2 quarts oil for deep frying
- 4 large apples, peeled and cored
- 1/2 cup confectioners' sugar for dusting

DIRECTION

1. Combine salt, flour, nutmeg, baking powder, and sugar in a medium bowl. Whisk milk and eggs together in another bowl. Combine the two bowls of mixture together until smooth. Pour oil in a skillet, deep fryer, or deep pot; heat to 190°C (375°F). Cut apples into half-inch rings. Submerge sliced apples in batter and fry in batches until golden, flip once. Place on paper towels to drain. Sprinkle confectioners' sugar on top.

NUTRITION: Calories: 181 kcal Carbohydrate: 21.7 g Fat: 9.8 g Protein: 2.4 g Sodium: 179 mg

174. Vegan Oreo® Donuts

Preparation Time: 35 Minutes
Cooking Time: 15 Minutes
Servings: 6

INGREDIENTS

Cooking spray:

- 3/4 cup all-purpose flour
- 1/2 cup white sugar
- 1/4 cup cocoa powder
- 1/2 tsp. baking soda
- 1/4 tsp. salt
- 1/2 cup water
- 5 tbsps. vegetable oil
- 1/2 tsp. vanilla extract

Frosting:

- 2 1/2 cups confectioners' sugar
- 4 oz. vegan margarine
- 4 oz. shortening
- 2 tbsps. coconut milk
- 1/4 cup crushed chocolate sandwich cookies (Oreos)

DIRECTION

1. Preheat the oven to 175°C (350°F). Use cooking spray to grease a donut pan. Combine salt, flour, baking soda, cocoa powder, and sugar in a bowl. Mix in vanilla extract, vegetable oil, and water until smooth. Scoop batter in the donut pan. Place in the preheated oven and bake for 10-12 minutes until an inserted toothpick comes out dry. Let it cool for 10 minutes in a wire rack, inverted. In a big bowl, beat coconut milk, confectioners' sugar, shortening, and vegan margarine with an electric mixer until the mixture is smooth and fluffy. Pour frosting on top of the doughnuts, top with cookie crumbs.

NUTRITION: Calories: 762 kcal Carbs: 85.2 g Fat: 47.5 g Protein: 2.5 g Sodium: 369 mg

175. Funnel Cakes

Preparation Time: 10 Minutes

Cooking Time: 20 Minutes

Servings: 6

INGREDIENTS

- 8 cups vegetable oil for frying
- 1 1/2 cups milk
- 2 eggs
- 2 cups all-purpose flour
- 1 tsp. baking powder
- 1/2 tsp. ground cinnamon
- 1/2 tsp. salt
- 3/4 cup confectioners' sugar

DIRECTION

1. Pour oil a heavy skillet or deep fryer, heat to 190°C (375°F). Whisk eggs and milk in a big bowl. Mix together salt, flour, cinnamon, and baking powder; combine with the egg mixture until smooth. Use your hands to cover the funnel hole, add a cup of batter. Position the funnel over the skillet or fryer, uncover the funnel and swirl the batter starting at the middle. Form a 6-7-inch round and fry each side until golden. Place on a paper towel to drain. Dust with confectioners' sugar. Serve warm.

NUTRITION: Calories: 524 kcal Carbs: 50 g Fat: 32.6 g Protein: 8.4 g Sodium: 303 mg

176. Applesauce Doughnuts With Buttermilk

Preparation Time: 30 Minutes

Cooking Time: 50 Minutes

Servings: 24

INGREDIENTS

- 2 quarts oil for deep frying
- 3/4 cup white sugar
- 2 tbsps. butter, softened
- 2 eggs
- 3/4 cup applesauce
- 4 cups sifted all-purpose flour
- 2 tsps. baking powder
- 1 tsp. salt
- 1/2 tsp. baking soda
- 1/2 tsp. ground mace
- 1/2 tsp. ground cinnamon
- 1/2 cup buttermilk
- 1/4 cup confectioners' sugar for dusting

DIRECTION

1. Pour oil in a deep fryer and heat to 375°F (190°C). Combine applesauce, white sugar, eggs, and butter in a big bowl. Stir cinnamon, flour, mace, baking powder, baking soda, and salt in another bowl. Mix flour mixture, in turns with buttermilk, into the egg mix. Stir well until it forms into stiff dough. Roll dough evenly to 3/4 to an inch thick in a floured surface. Use a doughnut cutter to cut. Fry the donuts in heated oil until each side is golden brown, flip once they rise at the top. Place on paper towels to drain. Sprinkle confectioners' sugar on top and serve hot.

NUTRITION: Calories: 190 kcal Carbohydrate: 24.7 g Fat: 9 g Protein: 2.9 g Sodium: 172 mg

177. Banana Fritters

Preparation Time: 20 Minutes

Cooking Time: 30 Minutes

Servings: 10

INGREDIENTS

- 2 quarts oil for frying
- 1 cup all-purpose flour
- 1 1/4 tsps. baking powder
- 1/4 tsp. salt
- 1 egg, beaten
- 2 cups milk
- 2 tsps. canola oil
- 3 bananas, mashed
- 1 tbsp. lemon juice
- 2 tbsps. confectioners' sugar

DIRECTION

1. Pour oil in a deep fryer, heat to 190°C (375°F). Combine salt, baking powder, and flour in a big bowl. Beat egg, canola oil, and milk in another medium-sized bowl; combine into the flour mixture. Fold in lemon juice and bananas. Mix well and form into about 10 balls. Fry in hot oil for 5 minutes until slightly brown, work in batches. Place on paper towels to drain. Dust with confectioners' sugar on top.

NUTRITION: Calories: 279 kcal Carbs: 21.7 g Fat: 20.2 g Protein: 3.9 g Sodium: 131 mg

178. Beignets

Preparation Time: 30 Minutes

Cooking Time: 3 Hours

Servings: 10

INGREDIENTS

- 2 1/4 tsps. active dry yeast
- 1 1/2 cups warm water (110°F/45°C)
- 1/2 cup white sugar
- 1 tsp. salt
- 2 eggs
- 1 cup evaporated milk
- 7 cups all-purpose flour
- 1/4 cup shortening
- 1-quart vegetable oil for frying
- 1/4 cup confectioners' sugar

DIRECTION

1. Dissolve yeast in a big bowl of warm water; stir in evaporated milk, sugar, eggs, and salt. Add 4 cups flour and mix until smooth. Mix in the leftover 3 cups flour and shortening; cover. Let it chill in the refrigerator for a day, max. Spread out dough to 1/8 thick and cut to squares with 2 1/2-inch dimension. Fry the beignets in 180°C (360°F) oil. Make sure that the oil is hot enough for the beignets to pop up. Place on paper towels to drain. Dust confectioners' sugar on top of hot beignets. Serve.

NUTRITION Information: Calories: 543 calories; Carbs: 82.7 g Fat: 17.7 g Protein: 12.4 g Sodium: 277 mg

179. Buttermilk Doughnuts

Preparation Time: 20 Minutes

Cooking Time: 25 Minutes

Servings: 36

INGREDIENTS

- 2 cups vegetable oil for frying
- Doughnuts:
- 2 cups buttermilk
- 1 cup white sugar
- 2 large eggs, beaten

Glaze:

- 3 cups confectioners' sugar
- 1 tbsp. margarine, softened (optional)
- 1/2 tsp. vanilla extract
- 2 tbsps. milk, or as needed
- 5 cups sifted all-purpose flour
- 2 tsps. baking soda
- 1 tsp. baking powder
- 1 tsp. salt
- 1 tsp. ground nutmeg
- 1/4 tsp. ground cinnamon
- 1/2 cup melted butter

DIRECTION

1. In a deep-fryer or big saucepan, heat oil to 375°F (190°C). Mix buttermilk, eggs and sugar in a bowl. In a separate bowl, mix together flour, salt, nutmeg, baking soda, baking powder, and

cinnamon. Combine buttermilk mixture with the flour mixture and mix until blended; add butter. Knead until a soft dough pulls together. Roll dough up to 1/4-inch thick on a slightly floured work surface. Using a 2 1/2-inch doughnut cutter, cut doughs into doughnuts. Whisk margarine, confectioner's sugar and vanilla extract in a mixing bowl until smooth. Pour milk little by little, continuously stirring, until your preferred glaze consistency is achieved. Fry doughnuts (by batch) in hot oil for 1 minute each side or until color turns golden brown. Place cooked doughnuts to a dish lined with paper towel to drain. Glaze doughnuts to coat.

NUTRITION: Calories: 172 kcal Carbs: 30 g Fat: 4.7 g Protein: 2.7 g Sodium: 189 mg

180. Cheese Fritters

Preparation Time: 15 Minutes

Cooking Time: 25 Minutes

Servings: 10

INGREDIENTS

- 1 cup drained cottage cheese
- 1 egg
- 1/4 cup half-and-half
- 1 cup all-purpose flour
- 1 3/4 tsps. baking powder
- 1/4 tsp. salt
- 2 tbsps. white sugar
- 1 tsp. ground nutmeg
- 4 cups vegetable oil for frying
- 3 tbsps. confectioners' sugar

DIRECTION

1. Whisk together egg and cottage cheese in a medium sized bowl. Mix in nutmeg, half-and-half, sugar, baking powder, and salt until well combined. Pour oil in a deep pot up to 2-in deep and heat to 190°C (375°F). Scoop rounded tablespoonful's of batter in hot oil. Fry for 3-4 minutes until all sides are golden brown. Place on paper towels to drain. Dust with confectioners' sugar and serve hot.

NUTRITION: Calories: 883 kcal Carbs: 15.7 g Fat: 90.4 g Protein: 4.9 g Sodium: 244 mg

181. Churros

Preparation Time: 30 Minutes

Cooking Time: 50 Minutes

Servings: 24

INGREDIENTS

- 1 1/4 cups hot water
- 1 1/2 cups buttermilk biscuit mix
- 4 cups vegetable oil for frying
- 1/2 cup white sugar
- 1 tbsp. ground cinnamon

DIRECTION

1. On medium-high heat, pour vegetable oil in a deep-frying pan up to 1 1/2 -in deep. Mix together baking mix and water in a bowl; beat for 3-4 minutes with a wooden spoon until it becomes even and spongy. In a pastry bag filled with batter, squeeze 5-in strips in hot oil. Fry until golden, best work in batches. Place on paper towels to drain. Combine cinnamon and sugar in a saucer or small bowl. Roll churros in the sugar mixture. Serve warm.

NUTRITION: Calories: 81 kcal Carbs: 9.1 g Fat: 4.8 g Protein: 0.6 g Sodium: 96 mg

182.   Coffee & Cream Doughnuts

Preparation Time: 10 Minutes

Cooking Time: 30 Minutes

Servings: 10

INGREDIENTS

- Oil for deep-fat frying
- 2 tubes (10.2 oz. each) large refrigerated buttermilk biscuits
- 1/4 cup heavy whipping cream
- 1 tbsp. plus 1 tsp. instant coffee granules
- 6 oz. cream cheese, softened
- 2/3 cup Nutella
- Confectioners' sugar and baking cocoa

DIRECTION

1. Heat oil in a deep fryer or electric skillet to 375°F. Fry a couple of biscuits at a time until each side is golden and brown. Place on paper towels to drain. In a microwavable bowl, put cream and microwave on high for a minute without a cover. Mix in coffee granules until dissolved. Whisk in Nutella and cream cheese until smooth. Make a small hole at the bottom edge of a plastic or pastry bag, put in a small tip. Put the coffee mixture inside the bag. Fill each donut with cream by inserting the tip at one side. Cover doughnut tops with cocoa and confectioners' sugar. Serve.

NUTRITION: Calories: 413 kcal Carbs: 37 g Fat: 28 g Protein: 7 g Sodium: 659 mg

183. Drop Doughnuts

Preparation Time: 10 Minutes

Cooking Time: 35 Minutes

Servings: 36

INGREDIENTS

- 1/2 cup mashed potatoes (mashed with milk and butter)
- 1/4 cup sugar
- 1 egg, lightly beaten
- 1/2 cup sour cream
- 1/2 tsp. vanilla extract
- 1-1/2 cups all-purpose flour
- 1/2 tsp. baking soda
- 1/4 tsp. baking powder
- Oil for deep-fat frying
- Additional sugar or confectioners' sugar, optional

DIRECTION

1. Combine together in a large bowl the vanilla, sour cream, egg, sugar and potatoes. Mix dry ingredients; add in potato mixture. Use electric skillet or deep-fat fryer and turn on to 375 degrees to heat the oil. Put teaspoonfuls of batter, a little at a time, into hot oil. Cook until both sides are golden brown in color. Use paper towels to drain on; rotate in sugar while it is still hot.

NUTRITION: Calories: 88 kcal Carbs: 11 g Fat: 4 g Protein: 2 g Sodium: 59 mg

184. Fluffy Cake Doughnuts

Preparation Time: 20 Minutes

Cooking Time: 30 Minutes

Servings: 12

INGREDIENTS

- 2 cups all-purpose flour
- 3/4 cup white sugar
- 2 tsps. baking powder
- 1/4 tsp. ground nutmeg
- 1/4 tsp. ground cinnamon
- 1 tsp. salt
- 3/4 cup milk
- 2 eggs, beaten
- 1 tsp. vanilla extract
- 1 tbsp. shortening
- 1 cup confectioners' sugar
- 2 tbsps. hot water
- 1/2 tsp. almond extract

DIRECTION

1. Preheat the oven to 165°C (325°F). Grease the doughnut pan lightly. Mix salt, flour, cinnamon, sugar, nutmeg, and baking powder in a big bowl. Stir in shortening, milk, vanilla, and eggs until well combined. Pour batter in doughnut cups until about three-fourths full. Bake in the preheated oven for 8-10 minutes until the tops are bouncy when touched. Let it cool, take the doughnuts out of the pan. In a small bowl, combine almond extract, hot water, and sugar for the glaze. Submerge donuts in glaze; serve.

NUTRITION: Calories: 196 kcal Carbs: 39.9 g Fat: 2.4 g Protein: 3.7 g Sodium: 272 mg

CHAPTER 10: FRUIT PRESERVES

185.   Christmas Jam

Preparation Time: 25 Minutes

Cooking Time: 35 Minutes

Servings: 14 half-pints

INGREDIENTS

- 1 package (40 oz.) frozen unsweetened strawberries, thawed or 2-1/2 quarts fresh strawberries, hulled

- 1 lb. fresh or frozen cranberries, thawed

- 5 lbs. sugar

- 2 pouches (3 oz. each) liquid fruit pectin

DIRECTION

1. In a grinder or food processor, grind cranberries and strawberries; put into a Dutch oven. Put in sugar. Bring to a full rolling boil; boil for 1 minute. Discard from the heat; stir in pectin and return to a full rolling boil. Boil, stirring constantly, about one minute. Discard from heat. Let cool for 5 mins; remove the foam. Ladle the hot mixture carefully into the hot half-pint jars, remaining 1/4-inch headspace. Discard the air bubbles, then wipe the rims and adjust the lids. Process in the boiling-water canner for 10 mins.

NUTRITION: Calories: 84 kcal Carbs: 22 g

186.   Apple Pie Jam

Preparation Time: 30
Cooking Time: 40
Servings: 7 half-pints

INGREDIENTS

- 4 to 5 large Golden Delicious apples, peeled and sliced (about 2 lbs.)
- 1 cup water
- 5 cups sugar
- 1/2 tsp. butter
- 1 pouch (3 oz.) liquid fruit pectin
- 1-1/2 tsps. ground cinnamon
- 1 tsp. ground nutmeg
- 1/4 tsp. ground mace, optional

DIRECTION

1. Mix water and apples in a Dutch oven. Put on the cover and slowly cook till soft. Get 4-1/2 cups of the apples; put back to the pan. Set the rest of the apple mixture aside for other use or throw away. Mix in butter and sugar. On high heat, let it come to a full rolling boil, mixing continuously. Mix in the pectin. Keep boiling for a minute, mixing continuously. Take off the heat; skim off froth. Mix in spices. Into 7 of 1/2-pint hot jars, carefully ladle hot mixture, leaving a quarter-inch headspace. Get rid of air bubbles and adjust headspace, if needed, by putting in hot mixture. Wipe the rims. Put lids on top middle of jars; screw the bands on till fingertip tight. Into the canner of simmering water, put the jars, making sure that they are fully covered in water. Boil; let it process for 10 minutes. Take out the jars and let it cool.

NUTRITION: Calories: 76 calories Total Carbohydrate: 20 g Sodium: 1 mg

187. Delightful Fruit Compote

Preparation Time: 10 Minutes

Cooking Time: 10 Minutes

Servings: 8

INGREDIENTS

- 2 medium ripe peaches, sliced
- 1 cup fresh or frozen blueberries
- 1 cup quartered fresh strawberries
- 2 kiwifruits, peeled and sliced
- 3/4 cup seedless red or green grapes
- 3 tbsps. apple jelly
- 4 tsps. water
- Vanilla yogurt and sliced almonds, optional

DIRECTION

1. Mix grapes, kiwi, berries and peaches in a bowl. Mix water and jelly in a microwave-safe bowl; on high, microwave for 45 seconds till jelly melts, uncovered. Mix till smooth; drizzle on fruit. Put yogurt over the top; if desired, sprinkle with almonds.

NUTRITION INFORMATION: Calories: 80 kcal Carbs: 20 g Fiber: 2 g Protein: 1 g Sodium: 5 mg

188. Four-berry Spread

Preparation Time: 20 Minutes

Cooking Time: 30 Minutes

Servings: 7 half-pints

INGREDIENTS

- 1 cup fresh or frozen blackberries
- 1 cup fresh or frozen blueberries
- 1-1/2 cups fresh or frozen strawberries
- 1-1/2 cups fresh or frozen raspberries
- 1 package (1-3/4 oz.) powdered fruit pectin
- 7 cups sugar

DIRECTION

1. Crush the berries inside the Dutch oven. Mix in the pectin. Bring the mixture to a full rolling boil, stirring it often over high heat. Mix in the sugar. Bring the mixture to a full rolling boil and boil it for a minute while constantly stirring it. Remove it from the heat, skimming off any foam from the mixture. Ladle the hot mixture carefully into the hot half-pint jars, leaving only a headspace of 1/4-inch. Remove some air bubbles from the jars. Wipe the rims of the jars and adjust their lids. Process the jars in a boiling-water canner for 10 minutes.

NUTRITION: Calories: 107 kcal Carbs: 27 g Fiber: 1 g

189. Blackberry Jam

Preparation Time: 10 Minutes

Cooking Time: 1 Hour 30 Minutes

Servings: 16

INGREDIENTS

- 4 cups blackberries
- 1 cup white sugar
- 2 tbsps. cornstarch
- 1/4 tsp. ground cinnamon
- 1/4 tsp. ground allspice
- 1/2 tsp. lemon juice

DIRECTION

1. Use a potato masher to mash blackberries in the saucepan; mix in sugar till juices form. Put 1 tbsp. blackberry juice into a small bowl; mix in cornstarch. Put cornstarch mixture in a saucepan. Boil berries for 15 minutes till jam is thick, mixing often. Mix in allspice and cinnamon; take off from the heat. Cool. Put jam in a bowl and cover; refrigerate till chilled. Mix in lemon juice.

NUTRITION INFORMATION: Calories: 68 kcal Carbs: 16.9 g Fat: 0.2 g Protein: 0.5 g Sodium: < 1 mg

190. Blueberry and Raisin Jam

Preparation Time: 10

Cooking Time: 35

Servings: 10

INGREDIENTS

- 12 oz. raisins
- 1/2 cup orange juice
- 4 pints fresh blueberries
- 1 (1.75 oz.) package powdered low-sugar pectin
- 4 cups white sugar

DIRECTION

1. In a food processor or blender, process the orange juice and raisins till smooth; turn out the mixture onto a pot. In a food processor or blender, process blueberries until pureed; put into mixture of raisin. Into the fruit mixture, mix pectin and boil. Stir sugar into the fruit mixture; let it boil for approximately an additional of 5 minutes, mixing frequently, till sugar dissolves. In boiling water, sterilize the lids and jars for 10 minutes. Into the sterilized, hot jars, pack the jam, filling jars to within a quarter-inch of the surface. Trace a thin spatula or knife surrounding the inner of jars once filled to get rid of any air bubbles. Using a damp paper towel, wipe jars rims to get rid any food residue. Put lids on top, and screw the rings on. In a big stockpot bottom, put a rack and fill with water midway. Boil and into the boiling water, lower jars with a holder. Keep a 2-inch gap among the jars. Put in additional boiling water if needed to reach water level to a minimum of an-inch over the jar tops. Let water come to a rolling boil, put on the pot cover, and let it process for 10 minutes. Take jars out of stockpot and put onto a wood or cloth-covered surface, a few inches away, till cool. When cool, with a finger, press the surface of every lid, making sure that seal is tight, lid must not flex up or down at all. Keep in a dark cool place.

NUTRITION: Calories: 507 kcal Carbs: 131.5 g Total Fat: 0.6 g Protein: 2.1 g Sodium: 15 mg

CONCLUSION

Making these desserts at home will be a good and fun experience for you.

Adding fruits into your desserts is a benefit no matter how you look at it. Dessert that paired with fruits they actually make excellent desserts, delicious, moist and fragrant, and a great addition to every meal. Whether it is a regular dinner or a party with your family or friends, a dessert based on a fragrant fruit will surely impress and end the meal on a high note. In the end, the dessert is the one that can make or break a meal, isn't this what they say?!

If we extend the main idea of this book to your entire lifestyle, you will learn that fruits have their place into one's diet for a reason. I am sure you still remember when your mum was trying to make you eat your fruits and you couldn't understand then why was she so persistent. And I am also sure that you do the same now with your kids, just because fruits are healthy, they are little miracles of nature and one of the best ways to ensure we have a healthy and balanced diet and we get all the nutrients we need for a healthy body and mind.

The truth is there is nothing that works better than a healthy and balanced diet using fresh and healthy ingredients. Luckily, more and more people see this so if you are one of those people, congratulations! It is definitely not an easy step, but it is wise and shows that you are brave enough to go against the flow and eat healthy. And because we all have a sweet tooth and often feel guilty when eating desserts just because we believe they are far from being the healthiest things in the world.

You will about the benefits of fruits and their uses in desserts. Even though you will see that some of the recipes contain butter, keep in mind that butter has been around forever and our ancestor have been using it in their food for thousands of years. A small amount of butter is actually good for your health. Did you know that butter is rich in vitamin A, D and E? Did you know that it has selenium and lecithin which help keep our memory fit? In fact, butter is compulsory for kids as their brain needs that kind of fat to develop properly. The acids found in butter improve and help digestion and boost your immune system. Butter also has a perfect balance of omega-3 and omega-6 fats and despite what you may think or health, the cholesterol found in butter is good for your intestinal health, brain and nervous system, as long as it is being consumed with moderation.

Dessert also makes you feel good. You're in bad mood? Eat ice cream. You're stress? Go! Make a cupcake. Dessert is also good in all occasion. Valentine Day? Bake a cookie for your boyfriend or girlfriend. Birthday? Bake a cake for the celebrant. Everyone deserves sweetness in their lives.